Keto in an Instant

Keto in an Instant

More Than 80 Recipes *for* Quick & Delicious Keto Meals Using Your Pressure Cooker

Jen Fisch

HARPER WAVE
An Imprint of HarperCollinsPublishers

HarperCollins books may be purchased for educational, business, or sales promotional use. For information, please email the Special Markets Department at SPsales@harpercollins.com.

FIRST EDITION

All photographs credited to Leslie Grow.

Library of Congress Cataloging-in-Publication Data has been applied for.

ISBN 978-0-06-297324-5 (pbk.)

20 21 22 23 24   LSC   10 9 8 7 6 5 4 3 2 1

To my daughter, Kaia: You will always be my Chief Taste Tester and my reason for everything. I love you.

Contents

Introduction

If you've picked up this book, chances are you already know a thing or two about the ketogenic lifestyle. Maybe you're an old hand at this and you're looking for some new inspiration to create delicious meals. Or maybe you are brand-new to this keto thing and you're hoping to learn more about the ground rules—as well as how to cook for your family (whether they're keto or not). No matter where you are on your keto journey, I have good news: you've come to the right place!

Why should you listen to me? Well, I've been keto for four years, and in that time I've also become focused on recipe development and cookbook writing. I've written three previous keto cookbooks that are all focused on making the ketogenic lifestyle less intimidating through simple and delicious recipes with easy-to-find ingredients. What my readers and followers consistently want more of are recipes that can be thrown together quickly. They want meals they can make on a busy weeknight that don't require a laundry list of ingredients and that won't break their budget.

I get it. I'm a single working mom. I don't have a lot of time for meal prep and cooking. Every day after I send my teenage daughter off to school, I get in the car and drive an hour through LA traffic to work. At the end of the day, I weave back through traffic to pick her up from sports practice. When we get home it's dark, we're tired, and we're HUNGRY! So, dinner better be super fast and super satisfying.

When the Instant Pot first became popular, I was skeptical—it seemed like just another gadget. But when I finally gave it a try, I couldn't believe how much time it saved me. I could do maybe ten minutes of meal prep before leaving for work, throw everything in the Instant Pot when we got home in the evening, and by the time my daughter was done with her post-practice shower, a delicious dinner was ready to be served. It was amazing! I couldn't believe how quickly and easily our meals came together. I decided to focus on developing more recipes that could be made with this amazing appliance for my next book.

I realize that some people may be a little nervous to use a pressure cooker—I was intimidated by it when I first got one. It seemed strange to just throw in a bunch of ingredients, lock it up, and hope for the best. What if the food doesn't cook all the way through? What if the whole thing explodes? But trust me, if you follow the directions, your food will cook perfectly. Eventually I learned these appliances are super safe and basically foolproof.

In this book you'll find eighty of my most creative, inventive, rigorously tested recipes made with only keto-friendly ingredients. All of them can be cooked in the Instant Pot and made by anyone, regardless of your culinary skill level or confidence in the kitchen. I love showing people that keto doesn't need to be complicated. In fact, I think the simpler the recipe, the more delicious. No need to get all extra cheffy (unless you want to), and absolutely no need to splurge on fancy ingredients (unless you want to). In my recipes, I aim to use as few ingredients as possible, and I focus on building big, bold flavors that satisfy your cravings and leave you feeling energized and satiated rather than weighed down.

You'll find options for every major meal and category of protein (beef, pork, chicken, seafood) along with plenty of kid- and family-friendly recipes (Strawberry Cinnamon Rolls, anyone?) that will win over even the pickiest eaters. All of the recipes in this cookbook are gluten-free, as keto is inherently gluten-free, unless you add processed foods or sauces. I also provide easy swaps that allow you to make many of the recipes dairy-free if you wish. My goal is to share with everyone the life-changing benefits of a ketogenic lifestyle and make it easier than ever not only to reap the benefits of improved health, but also to enjoy yourself along the way.

Here's to your health!

xoxo

Jen

Chapter 1

How to Go Keto

There are a lot of different reasons to follow a ketogenic lifestyle: some people have health concerns like type 2 diabetes; others have food intolerances or allergies; some are simply looking to drop a little weight and get healthier in the process. My keto journey began as a way to control the chronic, systemic inflammation that had taken over my whole body. I am one of the more than fifty million Americans who suffer from an autoimmune disease, a disorder in which the body's immune system attacks healthy tissue, generating widespread inflammation. Common autoimmune disorders include type 1 diabetes, psoriatic and rheumatoid arthritis, lupus, Hashimoto's thyroiditis, celiac disease, and inflammatory bowel disease. At the time I was experiencing the painful symptoms of two autoimmune disorders, psoriatic arthritis and psoriasis. I've struggled with these issues for more than twenty years, and along the way I've discovered that the food I eat (and don't eat) can be a powerful complement to the treatment plan my doctors prescribe.

The first time I connected food to inflammation was more than a decade ago, when a doctor recommended I stop eating sugar. He explained that sugar creates a lot of inflammation in the body, and that everyone would benefit from cutting it out—but especially someone like myself who was battling autoimmune disorders. Prior to this I'd never even thought about how food might affect my skin or joints. So I took his advice. I started doing research and discovered that a lot of the foods I was eating regularly were high in sugar. I figured it was worth a shot, so I gave up sugar and cut down on carbohydrates, which quickly convert to sugar in the body. Within a couple weeks I noticed the redness in my skin had lessened and overall my body was less inflamed and "angry." Changing the way I ate wasn't a cure-all, but it made a noticeable difference.

I followed a low-carb diet for the majority of the next ten years, but I would definitely go off my plan fairly often—when a coworker brought in donuts, or my daughter wanted to go out for pizza, or a holiday or special celebration came up. Eventually, those occasional "treats" became more frequent, and before I knew it I was pretty much eating a standard diet. I was on a biologic medication that helped to control flare-ups in my skin and joints, but around this time I started having stomach issues. Gut inflammation was new to me, and I didn't know what to do about it. I went to the doctor for testing, but my results were inconclusive. My doctor suspected I might have Crohn's disease, but he couldn't make a definitive diagnosis. I decided to go back to basics and again focus on cleaning up my diet.

I returned to my low-carb/no sugar plan, but this time I also cut out gluten. My gut immediately felt better. Soon after that I started seeing the word *ketogenic* here and there, and the more I read about it, the more it made sense to me—it dovetailed with the style of eating that seemed to keep my inflammation at bay. It felt like an approach that could heal my body, keep me satisfied, and be sustainable for the long term.

If you live with other people, then you know how hard it can be to change the way you eat. When your roommate, partner or spouse, or kids keep sugary, high-carb food lying around, chances are good you'll get derailed. When I decided to go all-in on keto, I did a clean sweep and threw away everything in my house that wasn't keto-friendly. My daughter was ten at the time, and I decided that I just couldn't have her treats and snacks in the pantry—so when I went keto, she went keto! Besides, I don't have the time or energy to cook multiple meals every day—what Mama is eating, she is eating.

In my early days of being keto, there were a lot fewer resources available than there are now. The recipes I found online were complicated and tended to have a huge list of ingredients, half of which I didn't recognize. It was really disappointing, because part of what had appealed to me about the keto lifestyle was that I could eat simple food—grab a protein, grab butter or another healthy fat, grab a veggie, and BOOM: meal made! I had no interest in following an elaborate recipe. I was determined to make this lifestyle work for me and my daughter, and so I started creating my own recipes. I found that I loved expressing my creativity in the kitchen.

In the years since I went keto, my health has improved dramatically. One of the main improvements has been the quality of my sleep. Sleep is so key in allowing your body to recover, and when you have autoimmune issues it's critical. I was also able to lose forty pounds and keep it off, which has me feeling more energetic and helps my joints by not making them carry around excess weight. And of course the anti-inflammatory benefits were why I started my ketogenic journey in the first place, and it has made a huge difference for me. I have a form of arthritis that requires medication, and there have been times during my journey that my medicines have stopped working. I often need to rely on keeping my inflammation down with my food choices while I waited for a new medication to kick in. During those times it becomes really clear just how much the ketogenic lifestyle has helped me and improved my life.

Keto has become a way of life in my home, and I never want to turn back. I've seen so many people's lives changed for the better by living a ketogenic lifestyle. I encourage you to give it a try. I hope it's as powerful and beneficial for you as it has been for me!

Keto 101

If you're a keto newbie, WELCOME! While this lifestyle isn't hard to understand or maintain, it does require a little education initially so that you set yourself up for success. Over the last four years I've received thousands of questions from my Instagram and blog followers who are curious to try keto, and those questions form the basis of this chapter. So, without further ado, let's dive in!

What is keto?

You might know the basics already, but to put it very simply: The ketogenic diet is one that is high in fat, moderate in protein, and low in carbohydrates. When you restrict carbs drastically enough (typically 20 to 50 grams net carbs per day), your body naturally goes into a state of ketosis. It can take anywhere from a few days to a week or so of restricting carbs to achieve ketosis.

What is ketosis? It's the metabolic state in which our bodies turn to stored fat (ketones) as a primary source of fuel rather than glucose. When you remove carbs from your diet, your liver converts fat into fatty acids and ketones. Being in ketosis offers a lot of benefits, many of which you will start to experience in a matter of days—including increased energy, weight loss, mental clarity, and improved sleep.

A common misconception about following a keto diet is that all food fits neatly into one of two categories: "keto" or "not keto." If you spend time on keto social media pages you'll quickly notice the "keto police" commenting on whether this food or that food qualifies as keto. What I would encourage you to keep in mind is that food is not inherently keto or not—you are in control of keeping your body in ketosis, and the combination of foods you eat to make that happen will look a little bit different for everyone. The only way you'll know for sure if you're maintaining ketosis is if you take a test (see page 13 for details on how to test for ketosis), but I can tell you that once you're a month or two into your keto journey, you will know intuitively—your energy level, mental clarity, and feelings of hunger or satiety are all clues as to whether or not your body is burning fat for fuel.

What are macros and do they matter?

This was a subject that really confused me when I first started keto. Some people track macro-nutrients, or "macros" (fats, carbohydrates, and proteins), religiously, and some people don't track them at all. To put it simply, your daily calorie intake should break down into ratios that are very low in carbs, moderate in protein, and high in healthy fats. You'll ultimately need to determine what combination of macros works best for you, but traditional keto ratios are 5 to 10 percent carbs, 20 to 25 percent protein, and 70 to 75 percent fat. There are a lot of macro calculators online, and they take into account your size, gender, activity level, and goals, and provide you with target numbers. My macros are not the same as yours, so I recommend using one of these calculators and seeing what results you get. Then you can decide how closely you want to use those numbers as a guideline.

The most important calculation is your carb count. Keep that low and you will find success. The fat and protein ratios can be adjusted and refined over time as you find a lifestyle that works for you. While a lot of people want to know exactly what to eat and when, I've found the longer you go, the more in tune you are with your body's needs, and you know best how to meet them. It's also important to understand that you don't need to keep eating just to "hit your macros." If you're full, stop eating. Always try to stay under your carb goal and look at the protein and fat ratios as guidelines. If it's 8 p.m. and you're starving but have already eaten more than 100 grams of protein that day, then make sure you choose something high in fat and with little or no protein as a snack to satiate you. But if it's 8 p.m. and you aren't hungry, don't keep eating just to hit a macro number.

How many meals a day should I eat?

For most of our lives we've been told to eat three meals a day, but once I started following a ketogenic lifestyle, I found that wasn't really necessary for me. Most days I eat two meals, lunch and dinner, and just have coffee for breakfast. If I put a little fat in my coffee (like heavy cream, butter, ghee, or full-fat coconut milk), I'll be satisfied until lunch. Lunch tends to be my biggest meal most days, and then I'll have something a little lighter for dinner. But again, that's just what works for me and the logistics of my life. One of the great things about a keto lifestyle is that you can take your personal macros and design a plan tailored to your needs.

For example, let's say your macros goal is 1,800 total calories, with 99 grams fat; 90 grams protein; and 30 grams net carbs a day. You could eat three meals that are each made up of about 600 calories, with 33 grams fat, 30 grams protein, and 10 grams net carbs each; or you could eat two meals a day that are 900 calories, with 49.5 grams fat, 45 grams protein, and 15 grams net carbs each; or you could have one huge meal where you eat ALL THE FOOD! It's up to you! Your numbers will likely be different than these, but you get the point—you get to take your macros and design your day based on what makes sense for you.

Also, if you aren't hungry one day, *you don't need to eat at all*. One of the most important benefits of going keto is learning how to tune into what your body needs. Not every day has to look the same. Some days you'll be hungrier than others, and some days you may want to skip a meal or two. The best advice I can give you is to pay attention to what your body is trying to tell you and give it what it wants to function optimally.

You can also schedule your meals around special events (going keto doesn't mean you can't have fun anymore!). For example, if you have a special dinner out planned and you know you're going to order a nice, juicy steak with globs of butter, then you can choose to eat super light earlier in the day or skip lunch entirely. OMAD (one meal a day) is a fairly popular way of eating in the keto community because people find that the higher fat content in the foods they eat keeps them satisfied so they can fast for longer periods of time between meals.

What are net carbs?

When it comes to macros, some people go by *total* carbs, and some people go by *net* carbs. To get the net carb quantity for any given food, you simply take the total grams of carbs and subtract the grams of fiber. For example, 1 cup of broccoli has 6 grams of total carbs, but 2 grams of fiber, so the net carb count would be 4 grams. Whether you choose to use total or net carbs is a personal choice, but the nice thing about counting net carbs is it allows you to eat more high-fiber foods, and fiber is an important part of a healthy diet. I eat a lot of veggies as a part of my keto lifestyle, so just tracking net carbs works best for me. When it comes to recipes in the sweets chapter, you will also subtract the erythritol from the total carbs and see that called out as a separate line in the nutritional calculation. Erythritol is a sugar alcohol that doesn't create an insulin spike in your body. It tastes and bakes like sugar would, allowing you to enjoy delicious but low-carb desserts.

Isn't eating a lot of fat bad for you?

Not all fats are created equal, so it's important to be mindful of the types of fats you consume on keto. You want to avoid refined fats and oils like canola and corn oil. You also want to avoid trans fats. You should aim to eat saturated fats from sources like ghee, grass-fed butter, sour cream, and coconut oil; monounsaturated fats from foods like avocados, olives, and macadamia nuts; polyunsaturated omega-3 fats from fatty fish like salmon; and medium-chain triglycerides (MCTs), which can be found in MCT oil or coconut oil.

A lot of people think you need to start piling on the fats when you go keto, adding extra butter or oil to every bite of food, but the reality is most of us already have extra fat (especially if weight loss is one of your goals) that our bodies can burn for fuel. So you can definitely choose fatty cuts of meat or fish, or eat an avocado a day, or enjoy a pat of grass-fed butter on your food—but you don't need to add unnecessary fat or force yourself to eat more of it just to "fill up your macros." Again, as time goes on, you will be better able to tune into your body's hunger signals and eat only until you are satiated.

What does a typical day of eating keto look like for you?

On weekdays I usually eat two meals per day. Most days I skip breakfast and drink coffee with heavy cream or Bulletproof coffee (coffee blended with grass-fed butter and MCT oil). This typically keeps me full until lunchtime.

On weekdays I mostly pick up my lunch from someplace near my office. One of the things I love about keto is that it's very easy to find foods that work for me just about anywhere. My favorite working lunch is a poke (raw fish) bowl loaded with salmon, avocado, and spring mix greens (hold the rice!). I also love a bunless burger or a Cobb salad with salmon on top (yes, I am a salmon addict). On days when I work from home, I generally cook a bigger meal so that my daughter and I can eat the leftovers that evening.

For dinner I typically break out my Instant Pot to whip up a meal in a matter of minutes. I usually aim for simple but flavorful combinations of meat, fish, or poultry and veggies. I also love making breakfast for dinner—some of my favorite recipes are the Mexican Chorizo and Zucchini Frittata with Avocado Pico (page 39) and Bacon-Cheddar Frittata with Tomato-Avocado Relish (page 51).

I'm not a big snacker, and I don't really recommend frequent snacking on a keto program, but when I do need a little extra hit of energy, macadamia nuts are my go-to choice.

What is the keto flu and how do I avoid it?

The "keto flu" is a detox period when your body is transitioning to burning fat rather than sugar as a fuel source. If you've been eating a fair amount of carbs your whole life, there will definitely be an adjustment period that may feel a little bit uncomfortable. Symptoms of the keto flu include lightheadedness, muscle cramps, nausea, headaches, and fatigue.

The key to making it through this period is to get electrolytes back in your system. You need lots of water, lots of quality salt (such as Himalayan pink salt, which contains more trace minerals than other types of salt), and to make sure you are getting potassium and magnesium through your food (or a combination of food and supplements). Rest is also important in the first month or so, because again, your body is making a big transition.

My daughter got hit pretty hard with the keto flu when she first made the switch. The answer for her was a combination of Powerade Zero, bone broth, and eating food sprinkled with Himalayan pink salt. Now some people will say, "What about the artificial sweeteners in Powerade Zero?!" It does have some undesirable ingredients in it, but its added electrolytes were a real lifesaver for my daughter. If you are struggling with symptoms of the keto flu and need the focus and energy to get through a tough school or work day, you might consider it.

My top strategies for getting through the keto flu include:

- **Water with added electrolytes** (such as Smartwater). Electrolyte supplements can also be helpful, both liquid versions and capsules.
- **Salt.** Processed carbs are full of salt, and when you stop eating them, your body will crave more salt. So salt your food but use a high-quality salt such as sea salt or Himalayan pink salt. Other ways to get salt include sipping broth or bone broth, taking a shot of pickle juice, or sprinkling a little pink salt in your water.
- **Potassium-rich foods.** Of course, high-sugar bananas are off limits, but avocados and spinach contain way more potassium than a banana!
- **Magnesium-rich foods**, including dark chocolate, nuts, artichokes, spinach, and fish.
- **Plenty of sleep**, to allow your body to rest and recover.

Is there a difference between being in ketosis and being "fat-adapted"?

Within one to two weeks of restricting carbs, your body will usually convert to a ketogenic state. It takes longer—usually a month or two—to become what's known as "fat-adapted." When you are in a fat-adapted state, your body not only is receiving the healing and fat-burning benefits of ketosis, but has also fully adapted ketosis as its default. This means that if you eat or drink something that momentarily causes you to slip out of ketosis, it's easier to slip back in. Slipping out of ketosis is just a reality unless you eat the same exact foods every single day. But once you're fat-adapted, it's generally easy to get back to ketosis within a day or two.

When you start a keto program, I recommend committing to at least sixty days eating strictly keto-friendly foods, because that's when the real magic starts happening. After sixty days you should be in a full-fledged fat-adapted state and will really start seeing all of the great benefits. So many people tell me they "tried keto for a week or two, but it didn't work." You have to give your body more time to adjust.

What is intermittent fasting, and do you have to do it to be keto?

Intermittent fasting (IF) requires that you abstain from eating for a certain amount of time—typically, a fast is defined as a twelve-hour period (or longer). It sounds difficult, but if you count the time you're sleeping it really isn't that challenging. Many people who practice intermittent fasting aim for an eighteen-hour fasting period. A typical IF ratio is 18:6, so eighteen hours of fasting and six hours of eating. My eating window is generally between noon and 8 p.m. each day. Sometimes I don't eat until 1 or 2 or even 3 p.m., so I will adjust my window accordingly.

You don't have to practice IF to be keto, but a lot of people who live a keto lifestyle do incorporate intermittent fasting. Why? Not only does fasting enhance all the benefits of keto, but it's also relatively easy to do once you're fat-adapted because you're just not as hungry as you used to be. If you are brand-new to keto, I strongly recommend waiting a few months until you're sure you are fat-adapted before incorporating IF. Not only will it be easier for you to maintain the fast physically, but it will also be less overwhelming mentally to take on one new protocol at a time. If you decide intermittent fasting is something you want to incorporate, it has a lot of great benefits including weight loss, increased brain function, and lowered risk for disease.

Does drinking alcohol throw you out of ketosis?

Everyone is different when it comes to what makes them slip out of ketosis, so the only way to know for sure is to test new foods and drinks and see how you feel. I am able to drink alcohol in moderation and stay in ketosis. Of course, the type of alcohol you choose makes a difference. My standard drink is a vodka soda or vodka diet tonic with lime wedges. Many spirits are low-carb; it's the mixers that get people in trouble. Wine is also fairly low in carbs, so I will enjoy a glass of red wine when I have room in my macros. I will say that being keto seems to intensify your body's response to alcohol—I feel super dehydrated after I've had a couple drinks.

Keep in mind that if you do choose to have a few drinks, your body will burn off the alcohol before it can continue to burn fat, so drinking will stall weight loss. The first time you test

drinking alcohol, I recommend testing your ketones (see page 13 for details) the next day to check and see if you are still in ketosis. If not, it should be relatively easy to get back in after a day or two of strict eating.

What is the difference between "lazy keto," "clean keto," and "dirty keto"?

I'm not sure where these terms originated, but I'm not a huge fan of them because I think they create division within the keto community. I'd rather we all just support one another on our own individual journeys. That being said, here's a quick rundown of what these labels generally refer to:

- **Lazy keto:** People who follow lazy keto don't track their food or macros. They eat foods that allow them to stay in ketosis, but they don't bother marking things down in apps or whatnot. For many people who have been practicing keto for a long time and know intuitively what works for them, "lazy" keto makes a lot of sense.
- **Clean keto:** People who eat clean keto avoid processed foods and stick to mostly whole foods. This can mean all organic produce, grass-fed meats, wild-caught fish, pasture-raised eggs, etc. This is obviously an ideal way of eating, but not practical for everyone's lifestyle or budget.
- **Dirty keto:** People who consider themselves eating dirty keto eat processed and packaged foods. They may purchase organic, grass-fed, wild-caught proteins sometimes, but they might also go to a drive-through and eat a bunless fast-food burger.

Which category do I fit into? I'm kind of a combination of all three. I'm "dirty" because I eat protein-style (bunless) burgers from In-N-Out at least once a week, I'll drink diet soda sometimes, and I also eat packaged keto cookies and snacks when I'm on the go. I'm "clean" because when I do cook at home, I buy the best-quality meat, fish, eggs, produce, and dairy I can afford. And I'm "lazy" because I haven't tracked my food in years!

Rather than trying to fit into any one of these categories, I strongly suggest doing what works for your lifestyle, budget, and goals. Everyone's keto journey is personal, and I believe you should do what allows you to achieve your goals without worrying about labels or judgment from the "keto police."

How do I test my ketones?

Ketones can be detected in urine, blood, and breath. If you decide you want to track your ketones, there are a few ways to go about it.

- **Urine strips:** This is the least expensive testing option. If you are in your first couple weeks of eating a ketogenic diet, they can be a helpful way of checking to see if you've reached ketosis. In my experience, once you're fat-adapted, the urine strips are no longer accurate. I only used them in the very beginning of my keto journey.
- **Blood testing:** This is considered the most accurate method of testing. It is also the most expensive, although more and more companies are beginning to offer affordable options. To use a blood test, you prick your finger and put the blood on a strip, just like you would to check your glucose. Anything higher than 0.5 mmol/l is considered to be in ketosis. When I was tracking consistently, I used this method.
- **Breathalyzer:** Breath monitors are very easy to use, and the newer models offer the ability to sync with smart technology and apps to track your results. I was sent one to try and really liked its accuracy and ease of use. These can be a little expensive up front, but you don't have to continue to buy strips or any other equipment.

As far as when to test, I always checked a couple hours after my last meal. You can also test in the morning before you've had anything to eat or drink; this will be your lowest measurement.

I think that just about covers the basics of going keto. I hope I've debunked any misinformation you may have picked up, and dispelled any fear you may have had about going keto. I want you to be excited to embark on your journey, because really, it is a lifestyle that can bring you a lot of joy. Now let's take a peek into your kitchen and get you set up for success!

Chapter 2

The Keto Kitchen

At the start of your keto journey, I recommend you go through all of your cabinets and drawers and do a clean sweep of your kitchen and pantry to ditch any foods that could possibly tempt you off your plan. That said, I'm not here to tell you that you need to restock with a bunch of fancy ingredients. Remember my mantra: *simple is better*. And when it comes to eating relatively clean keto, you don't need anything other than the essentials to create delicious, satisfying meals.

If you took a look around my pantry, you'd see that it's not fancy at all; I don't have a million different oils, seasonings, and ingredients. I'm also not the type of person who keeps a fully stuffed fridge and freezer at all times. It might be because there are only two people in my household, but also because I like to buy fresh food as I need it to prevent unnecessary waste.

So, what are the pantry staples you need to make the recipes in this book? Here's my baker's dozen list of must-haves:

Pantry List

1. **Himalayan pink salt:** I'm a big believer in using Himalayan pink salt to season all of my food. As I said earlier, it's important to get enough salt when you're keto, and pink salt is packed with more than eighty trace minerals. It also helps the body detoxify, boosts energy, and helps improve digestion.

2. **Organic black pepper:** Did you know that black pepper is a natural anti-inflammatory? It contains piperine, which is a bioactive compound that's a natural painkiller!

3. **Grass-fed butter or ghee:** You can usually use butter and ghee interchangeably in keto cooking. I call for one or the other in my recipes, but you can use whichever you prefer. If you are trying to limit your dairy intake, I recommend using ghee, which is lactose-free because all of the milk solids are removed during production. In both cases, look for grass-fed varieties; the flavor is much better and grass-fed butter has been found to contain CLA, which is a fatty acid linked to fighting cancer, preventing bone loss, and helping your body build muscle rather than store fat.

4. **Avocado oil:** Both avocado oil and olive oil contain healthy fats like omega-3 fatty acids, but avocado oil has a slightly higher concentration of fats. It also has a higher smoke point than olive oil, so it works well for high-heat cooking. If you only want to invest in one kind of oil, I would buy avocado oil since it is so versatile.

5. **Olive oil:** I like to use olive oil in certain recipes where I want the flavor of the oil to really come through. Unlike avocado oil, which has virtually no taste, olive oil can add a distinct flavor profile to dishes.

6. **Full-fat coconut milk and coconut cream:** Look for canned brands that don't use any stabilizers or preservatives.

7. **Sweeteners:** In this book I use erythritol and stevia. Erythritol comes in granular, powdered, and brown sugar varieties. Stevia comes in powder and liquid forms.

Because erythritol is a sugar alcohol, it's subtracted when you calculate your net carbs, so you will see that reflected in the nutritional information for each recipe.

8. **Almond flour and/or coconut flour:** I like having both flours on hand to create different textures in baked goods. They are not 1:1 replacements of each other, so I don't recommend swapping them out unless you're experienced in doing so. If you want to buy only one, or are allergic to one of them, here is the basic formula for conversion: 1 cup almond flour = ½ cup coconut flour + double the eggs called for + more liquid called for (heavy cream, water, coconut milk, etc.). To convert in the other direction and use almond flour instead of coconut flour, you will need a lot more almond flour and a lot less liquid and eggs due to the absorbency of coconut flour. Replace ¼ cup coconut flour with at least 1 cup almond flour and use one less egg for every ¼ cup coconut flour called for in the original recipe.

9. **Tamari, coconut aminos, or soy sauce:** Tamari is a gluten-free alternative to soy sauce. Coconut aminos are a soy-free and gluten-free alternative. I switched from soy sauce to coconut aminos when I went keto because I wanted to limit soy and gluten.

10. **Seasonings:** I use a few seasoning mixes over and over again in this book. Italian seasoning, taco seasoning, pumpkin pie spice, Cajun seasoning, everything bagel seasoning, Old Bay seasoning, chile-lime seasoning (like Tajín), and dry ranch dressing mix. Additional individual seasonings are used on a per-recipe basis, but everything should be easy to find at any grocery store.

11. **Pork rinds:** Crushed pork rinds make the best bread crumb alternative! There are companies that sell precrushed pork rinds, but I just crush my own in a food processor.

12. **Vegetable, chicken, and beef broth:** Liquid is essential to pressure cooking, so you want to make sure you have plenty of broth on hand. I never buy low-sodium, because the extra salt is fine when you're eating keto.

13. **Cooking spray:** I use coconut oil spray, but you can use whichever variety you prefer.

I also keep my list of must-have perishables somewhat limited and then pick up specialty ingredients as needed for certain recipes. I focus on buying the best ingredients I can for my

budget. If you have a great local farmers' market, that can be a great place to pick up your meat, veggies, and fruit for the week.

1. **Eggs:** Pasture-raised if you can; you want your yolks as orange as possible.

2. **Uncured bacon:** A lot of bacon is cured and has added sugars, so look for bacon that has no added nitrates or preservatives.

3. **Avocados:** One of my favorite ingredients and also one of the most temperamental, but if you get the timing right, a perfectly ripe avocado is magical.

4. **Cream cheese (or dairy-free alternative):** Cream cheese is a surprisingly versatile ingredient that you'll find in quite a few of my recipes.

5. **Sour cream (or dairy-free alternative):** For dips, sauces, and topping.

6. **Heavy cream:** If you're eating dairy on keto, you will use cream in many recipes. Buy grass-fed and organic if possible.

7. **Cauliflower:** Is there any high-carb dish that can't be successfully re-created with cauliflower? It's a super-versatile ingredient and my favorite vegetable.

8. **Greens:** It's important to eat plenty of leafy greens, which contain essential vitamins and minerals. Spinach and kale are my favorites.

9. **Meat:** Look for pastured and grass-fed and -finished whenever possible. It's really important to get the best quality you can find and afford.

10. **Seafood:** Look for wild-caught whenever possible. You can save money by purchasing your seafood frozen (Trader Joe's has some great options).

11. **Berries:** Low in sugar and high in fiber, these are a great fruit choice when you're on keto. Choose organic when possible.

12. **Green and black olives, pickles, capers, and pepperoncini:** Great for snacking, topping salads, and adding to recipes when you want a kick of flavor!

13. **Sugar-free chocolate:** This is a MUST HAVE and I use it a lot in my baking. I am obsessed with the ChocZero brand for sugar-free chocolate and syrup.

14. **Nuts:** Pecans, macadamia, and almonds are the nuts I use most often in my cooking.

15. **Cheese:** Another bonus of going keto: You can eat plenty of cheese! I buy various varieties, but Mexican blend and Parmesan are almost always in my fridge so that I can quickly add a melted, gooey layer to just about any dish.

Grocery Shopping

Going keto doesn't have to be expensive, especially if you're cooking the majority of your meals at home. Keto meals are also very filling, so you end up eating less food than you would eat on a standard diet, which helps to save you dollars at the grocery store. That said, it is important to look for the best-quality products you can afford. Because I started eating keto to fight inflammation, I would be doing myself a disservice if I ate a bunch of low-quality proteins and processed foods even if they were technically keto-friendly. Factory-farmed proteins are lower in nutrients and can contain hormones, antibiotics, nitrates, and preservatives that cause inflammation (and other issues) in the body.

If you're trying to figure out where you should splurge on organic ingredients and where you can save a little by buying conventionally raised or grown produce, I recommend using the Environmental Working Group's "Dirty Dozen" list as a guide. The Dirty Dozen are foods that have been found to contain the highest concentration of pesticide residue, so whenever possible you want to purchase organic varieties of these foods. Quite a few of these are not typically included in a ketogenic lifestyle, so I've highlighted the ones below that I use in my recipes.

THE DIRTY DOZEN

1. Strawberries
2. Spinach
3. Kale
4. Nectarines
5. Apples
6. Grapes
7. Peaches
8. Cherries
9. Pears
10. Tomatoes
11. Celery
12. Potatoes

Note: Hot peppers aren't technically part of the twelve but are known to have a lot of pesticides as well, so to be safe I would purchase organic here too. I also choose organic varieties of lettuce, cucumbers, and green beans.

Of course, in an ideal world, I would purchase all organic all the time, but I live in a realistic world where that is not always possible. Here's a list of the "Clean 15"—the conventionally raised produce that has been shown to have the least pesticide residue. I typically buy conventional versions of the items on this list—including avocados and cauliflower, which are staples of the keto diet. Again, I've highlighted those I use most often.

THE CLEAN 15

1. Avocado
2. Corn
3. Pineapple
4. Frozen sweet peas
5. Onions
6. Papaya
7. Eggplant
8. Asparagus
9. Kiwi
10. Cabbage
11. Cauliflower
12. Cantaloupe
13. Broccoli
14. Mushrooms
15. Honeydew melon

The Dirty Dozen and Clean 15 lists change every year, so be sure to check out ewg.org for updates.

Cooking Tools

Like my pantry items, I tend to keep my kitchen tools pretty simple. Obviously the most important tool you'll need is an electric pressure cooker such as the Instant Pot (more on that in the next chapter), but there are a few other staples I rely on for my cooking and baking. You probably have most of these already—if not, no need to invest unless you want to!

- **Food processor:** I use my food processor to make prep work easier. But as long as you have either a high-powered blender or a bullet blender instead, you'll be fine!
- **Immersion blender:** This works great for soups; but again, it isn't essential if you have another type of blender.
- **Silicone egg bite molds:** I love using these for individually sized egg bites that make breakfast so easy. The Double-Pork Egg Bites (page 44) are one of my favorites, and I also use these for my maple-bacon Pancake Bites (page 48)!
- **Ramekins:** I like to use 4-ounce and 6-ounce ramekins depending on the recipe—they are great for making single-serving desserts, egg dishes, and more.
- **3-cup Bundt pan:** This may not entirely be a staple, but it is very useful.
- **7-inch round baking dish:** The perfect size for my pressure cooker, this pan is used to make my Cinnamon-Pecan Coffee Cake (page 189) and many other recipes.
- **13 × 9-inch baking dish:** When I'm not using my pressure cooker, I'm probably using my Le Creuset baking dish. I love it and it was totally worth the investment.
- **13-inch nonstick deep sauté pan:** I don't use cast-iron pans because they are too heavy for my arthritic hands, so I stick to a great deep, nonstick sauté pan.
- **Steamer basket:** It seems strange to me that pressure cookers don't come with a steamer basket, but they don't, so you will definitely want to pick one up.

If this seems like a short list, that's intentional: You don't need a bunch of fancy equipment or pans to cook amazing meals. I've shared my favorites here to help you get inspired and organized, but by no means do you have to go to the store and spend a lot of money on a bunch of new stuff. As you continue your keto journey, you can reward yourself with a few new items or upgrades here and there.

Now let's take a closer look at the one kitchen tool that's essential to this cookbook: a pressure cooker!

Chapter 3

Pressure-Cooking Basics

A lot of people are nervous about using a pressure cooker for the first time, but I promise, it's easier than you think. In fact, my electric pressure cooker is probably the easiest, most foolproof kitchen appliance I've ever used. Pressure-cooking makes cooking easy because there's very little prep, a short cook time, and barely any cleanup. Plus it's as easy to cook for two people as it is for eight, so it's a great option for anyone. And in fact, being able to cook in large quantities is helpful even if, like me, your household is pretty small. I'm able to batch-cook and freeze leftovers so that we always have meals on hand.

Of course, I know you'll have some questions about using the pressure cooker (just like I did when I started out!), and I'm happy to answer them. Here's a rundown of the questions I get asked most often by my readers.

Why should I buy a pressure cooker?

First and foremost, it is FAST! You can cook big pieces of meat in minutes instead of hours, and you can cook for a crowd without dirtying a million dishes. If, like me, you work long hours and are dead tired at the end of the day . . . the pressure cooker will be your new best friend. Just throw in your ingredients, seal it up, pour yourself a glass of wine, and dinner is ready by the time you're ready for glass number two!

The pressure cooker also helps infuse flavors into proteins really quickly, so your meal will taste like it was slow-roasted for hours. Last, but certainly not least, using the pressure cooker also makes post-meal cleanup a breeze!

What type of pressure cooker should I choose?

The recipes in this book will work with any electric pressure cooker, but I have an Instant Pot (IP). When I first got it I was a little bit intimidated by all of the various buttons and settings, but after I started using it, I found that I pretty much only use two settings: Sauté and Manual/Pressure Cook.

The Sauté function will brown and sear, and though you could do that in a pan on the stovetop, I like to do it in the Instant Pot so that I don't dirty a skillet. You can adjust the sauté temperature to low, medium, or high. The Manual/Pressure Cook (different models call it different things) setting is what you'll use most of the time. My IP is automatically on high pressure, but you can switch it to low if a recipe calls for it or if your electric pressure cooker model is different. You can also adjust the time needed based on the recipe.

Again, I rarely use the other settings, and while I encourage you to try them out, you won't need to learn about them to make the recipes in this book—even the soup recipes are cooked using the standard Manual/Pressure Cook mode. You will, however, use the Steam setting for veggies, especially for the recipes in Chapter 5.

I've never had luck with electric pressure cookers in the past. What am I doing wrong?

If you follow the recipes in this book, you should find success because they have all been tested and retested and tested again! However, there are some common mistakes that people make with pressure cookers. A lot of times it comes down to the liquid level; if your lid or the seal aren't on correctly, all the water can evaporate. The same thing can happen if you forget to switch from venting to sealing. Those are easy things to fix but can result in burned food if you don't catch them. Your pressure cooker needs liquid to do its thing, so triple-check you have set it correctly.

Another common issue people have is the sealing ring being damaged or broken. Sealing correctly is imperative to the pressure cooker working correctly. You might hear the hiss of steam leaking out if the seal is damaged. You can keep a couple of sealing rings on hand just in case.

Lastly, sometimes people make substitutions to recipes and this doesn't always work out. Maybe you used a bigger or smaller cut of protein than the recipe called for. Maybe you used almond flour instead of coconut flour. If you deviate from the recipe, I can't promise it will turn out perfectly. I strongly recommend following these recipes as closely as possible.

Will my cook times be different at high altitude?

Yes! For years I lived at high altitude in Boulder and Denver, Colorado, and then even higher in Santa Fe, New Mexico, and cooking was always a little trickier. Here are some general adjustments on how much time to add depending on just how high in the sky you are living!

- +5 to 10% at 3,000–4,000 feet
- +15 to 20% at 5,000–6,000 feet
- +25 to 30% at 7,000–8,000 feet
- +35 to 40% at 9,000–10,000 feet
- +45 to 50% at 11,000–12,000 feet

Should I use "quick release" or "natural release" when the dish is done?

The recipes will instruct you on which to use for each dish. Sometimes both will be used within a single dish. For "quick release," you turn the steam handle to the venting position to quickly release the steam. Be mindful that the steam is extremely hot, so take care to not open the vent with the steam facing you or anyone else. For a "natural release," let the pressure cooker slowly release the pressure on its own, until the float valve drops. The time varies for this based on how much food was cooked; it can sometimes take up to 40 minutes, but can also take as little as 10.

Two more safety tips before you start cooking:

1. Don't fill your pressure cooker more than about two-thirds full.
2. Make sure you let the pressure cooker finish releasing before you try to open it. Never try to force open a pressure cooker!

Hopefully I've put your mind at ease about the pressure cooker—it really will make your life easier, not harder. Now it's time to put everything together and step into the kitchen! The next eight chapters feature recipes that I developed specifically for electric pressure cooking. No matter what you're in the mood for, you'll find dishes to satisfy every craving imaginable. You don't need to be a seasoned cook to successfully make these dishes—my instructions are simple and foolproof, and each recipe is accompanied by a photo (if you're a visually oriented person like me, you know how helpful it is to see what your dish is supposed to look like). Let's get cooking!

Chapter 4

Breakfast

Strawberry Cinnamon Rolls

Cinnamon rolls hold such a happy place in my heart, and I've learned from readers of my past cookbooks that I'm not alone in that sentiment! The base of this recipe is "fathead dough," a keto staple that you can use to make all kinds of sweet and savory baked goods. For even more strawberry flavor, you can replace the sweetener with a tablespoon of sugar-free strawberry preserves.

1. Generously brush a 6-inch metal cake pan with a removable bottom with some melted butter. Set the pan aside.

2. Make the filling: In a small microwave-safe bowl, microwave the butter to melt, about 30 seconds. In a bowl, stir together the strawberries, erythritol, and cinnamon. Set the melted butter and the strawberry mixture aside.

3. Make the fathead dough: In a microwave-safe medium bowl, combine the mozzarella and cream cheese and microwave for 30 seconds. Stir and microwave another 30 seconds. Stir and add the egg and coconut flour and stir until well combined. Shape into a ball. (If the dough is sticky, sprinkle with a little additional coconut flour.)

4. Cut two 12-inch lengths of parchment paper and coat with cooking spray. Place the dough between them. Roll the dough into a 7 × 10-inch rectangle about ¼ inch thick. Peel off the top piece of parchment paper. Brush about 1 tablespoon of the reserved melted butter over the dough. Sprinkle with the strawberry filling, leaving a ½-inch border.

5. Starting from a short side, roll up the dough. Cut the roll crosswise into ten ½-inch-thick rolls. Arrange the rolls cut-side up in the prepared pan. Brush the roll tops with 1 tablespoon of the melted butter. Cover with two layers of paper towels, then tightly cover the top and bottom of the cake pan with foil.

6. Pour 2 cups water into the Instant Pot. Place a trivet with handles in the pot and place the pan on the trivet. Secure the lid on the pot and close the pressure-release valve. Set the pot to **HIGH** pressure for 25 minutes. At the end of the cooking time, use a natural release to depressurize. Remove the trivet from the pot and let the rolls cool 10 minutes before frosting.

Serves: 5
Active prep time: 30 minutes
Cook time: 25 minutes

Melted butter, for the cake pan

For the filling:
3 tablespoons butter or ghee
¾ cup finely chopped strawberries
2 tablespoons granular erythritol
2 teaspoons ground cinnamon

For the fathead dough:
¾ cup shredded mozzarella cheese (3 ounces)
2 tablespoons cream cheese
1 large egg, lightly beaten
¾ cup coconut flour

For the frosting:
4 tablespoons cream cheese, at room temperature
2 tablespoons butter, at room temperature
2 tablespoons heavy cream
1 tablespoon erythritol
¼ teaspoon vanilla extract

(continues)

7. Make the frosting: In a small bowl, use a fork to stir together the cream cheese, butter, heavy cream, erythritol, and vanilla. If necessary, stir in additional cream to reach a spreadable consistency. Spread frosting over the rolls before removing them from the pan. Serve warm.

Per serving: Calories: 330 · Total Fat: 27 g · Protein: 9 g · Total Carbs: 21 g · Fiber: 7 g · Erythritol: 7 g · Net Carbs: 7 g

Sausage and Mushroom Ramekin Eggs

Ramekin eggs are a simple dish that give you the opportunity to play with different flavor combinations. This version with sausage, mushrooms, and mozzarella is a classic, but you could swap in any meat, cheese, or vegetable you'd like. You can also opt to make these single-serving ramekins dairy-free by leaving out the cheese and swapping out the heavy cream for canned coconut milk (just be sure to shake it up or whisk it together before measuring). Personally, I love my eggs topped with some perfectly melted cheese!

10 INGREDIENTS OR LESS

Serves: 4
Active prep time: 10 minutes
Cook time: 5 minutes

Butter or ghee, for the
    ramekins
1 tablespoon avocado oil
4 ounces bulk breakfast
    sausage
1 cup chopped mushrooms
4 large eggs
Fine Himalayan pink salt and
    black pepper
4 tablespoons heavy cream
4 tablespoons shredded
    mozzarella cheese (1 ounce)

1. Coat the bottoms and sides of four 6-ounce ramekins with butter. Set aside.

2. Select **SAUTÉ** on the Instant Pot. When the pot is hot, add the avocado oil. Add the sausage and mushrooms to the hot oil and cook and stir until the sausage crumbles are browned and the mushrooms tender, about 5 minutes. Select **CANCEL**.

3. Remove the sausage and mushrooms from the pot and divide among the ramekins. Crack one egg into each ramekin and sprinkle with a pinch each of salt and black pepper. Add 1 tablespoon cream and top with 1 tablespoon mozzarella.

4. Pour 1 cup water into the Instant Pot. Place a trivet with handles in the pot and place three ramekins on the trivet. Stagger the remaining ramekin on top. Secure the lid on the pot and close the pressure-release valve. Set the pot to **HIGH** pressure for 5 minutes. At the end of the cooking time, quick-release the pressure. Open the pot and lift the trivet and ramekins from the pot.

Per serving: Calories: 282 • Total Fat: 25 g • Protein: 14 g • Total Carbs: 2 g • Fiber: 0 g • Erythritol: 0 g • Net Carbs: 2 g

Mexican Chorizo and Zucchini Frittata with Avocado Pico

I love the heat of chorizo, and it pairs perfectly with eggs and creamy avocado in this tasty frittata. This meal is super filling and can be enjoyed any time of day—it's just as delicious for dinner as it is for breakfast or brunch. The avocado pico is really the standout of this recipe—I add it to all kinds of dishes—and it makes for a nice keto-friendly "salsa" snack as well. If you're not a cilantro person, feel free to substitute fresh parsley.

1. Select **SAUTÉ** on the Instant Pot. When the pot is hot, add the olive oil. Add the chorizo to the hot oil and cook, stirring occasionally, until cooked through, about 5 minutes. Add the zucchini and cook and stir until crisp-tender, about 5 minutes more. Stir in the green onions. Select **CANCEL**.

2. Brush a 7-inch round baking dish with the softened butter.

3. In a medium bowl, whisk together the eggs and cream. Stir in the chorizo mixture and the cheese. Transfer to the prepared dish. Cover the dish tightly with foil.

4. Clean the pot. Pour 1 cup water into the Instant Pot. Place a trivet with handles in the pot and place the baking dish on the trivet. Secure the lid on the pot and close the pressure-release valve. Set the pot to **HIGH** pressure for 20 minutes. At the end of the cooking time, select **CANCEL**, even if your electric pressure cooker automatically switches to Keep Warm, and use a natural release to depressurize. Carefully remove the trivet and baking dish from the pot. Remove the foil and let stand for 10 minutes.

5. Meanwhile, make the avocado pico: In a medium bowl, combine the avocados, olive oil, cilantro, jalapeño, and lime juice. Season to taste with salt.

6. Serve the frittata with the pico.

Per serving: Calories: 532 • Total Fat: 47 g • Protein: 23.5 g • Total Carbs: 6 g • Fiber: 2.5 g • Erythritol: 0 g • Net Carbs: 3.5 g

Serves: 4
Active prep time: 15 minutes
Cook time: 20 minutes

1 tablespoon olive oil
1 pound Mexican chorizo sausage
1 medium zucchini, peeled, if desired, and chopped (about 2 cups)
2 green onions, chopped
1 tablespoon grass-fed butter, at room temperature
6 large eggs
½ cup heavy cream
1 cup shredded Monterey Jack or cheddar cheese (4 ounces)

For the avocado pico:

2 avocados, cut into bite-size pieces
2 tablespoons olive oil
½ cup coarsely chopped fresh cilantro
1 jalapeño pepper, minced
2 teaspoons fresh lime juice
Fine Himalayan pink salt or sea salt

Maple-Pecan Fathead Monkey Bread

Monkey bread is typically a sugar- and carb-rich bread made from refrigerated biscuit dough—all the little globs of dough piled together allow you to pull it apart and eat it in satisfying little chunks. I never thought I'd be able to enjoy this particular treat with a ketogenic lifestyle, but I'm here to tell you it is possible. This ooey-gooey breakfast is one of my daughter's absolute favorites.

10 INGREDIENTS OR LESS

Serves: 6
Active prep time: 15 minutes
Cook time: 22 minutes

¾ cup shredded mozzarella cheese (3 ounces)
2 tablespoons cream cheese
1 large egg, lightly beaten
¾ cup coconut flour
3 tablespoons granular erythritol
½ teaspoon ground cinnamon
4 tablespoons chopped pecans
3 tablespoons grass-fed butter or ghee
3 tablespoons ChocZero maple syrup (or sugar-free syrup of your choice)
½ teaspoon vanilla extract

1. Generously coat a 3-cup Bundt pan with cooking spray.

2. In a microwave-safe medium bowl, combine the mozzarella cheese and the cream cheese. Microwave on high for 30 seconds. Stir and microwave for 30 seconds more. Stir, then add the egg and coconut flour and stir until well combined. Use clean hands to shape into a ball. (If the dough is sticky, sprinkle with a little additional coconut flour.)

3. Cut two pieces of parchment paper and coat with cooking spray. Place the dough between the parchment and roll into a 6-inch square about ½ inch thick. Cut the dough into 24 pieces.

4. In a gallon-size resealable plastic bag, combine the erythritol and cinnamon. Add 8 pieces of dough and shake to coat. Arrange the coated pieces in the Bundt pan. Sprinkle with 2 tablespoons of the pecans. Repeat with the remaining spice mixture, dough pieces, and the remaining 2 tablespoons pecans. Make a final layer of dough.

5. In a small microwave-safe bowl, combine the butter and ChocZero. Microwave for 30 seconds or until the butter is melted and the mixture is bubbling. Stir in the vanilla. Pour over the dough mixture in the pan. Cover the pan with foil.

6. Pour 1 cup water into the Instant Pot. Place a trivet with handles in the pot and place the Bundt pan on the trivet. Secure the lid and close the pressure-release valve. Set the pot to **HIGH** pressure for 22 minutes. At the end of the cooking time, quick-release the pressure.

7. Carefully remove the pan from the pot. Cool the monkey bread in the pan on a wire rack for 10 minutes. Invert the bread onto a plate. Cool for 10 minutes.

Per serving: Calories: 250 • Total Fat: 22 g • Protein: 8 g • Total Carbs: 18 g • Fiber: 9 g • Erythritol: 6 g • Net Carbs: 3 g

Mediterranean Egg Salad Boats

I could eat egg salad for breakfast, lunch, and dinner. This Mediterranean-inspired version kicks up the flavor with Kalamata olives and feta cheese. I also use olive oil for a change from the usual mayo. If you prefer a creamier, more traditional egg salad texture, you can swap out the olive oil and lemon juice for ¼ cup avocado-oil mayonnaise. You can use either a scooped-out cucumber or crisp romaine leaves as the "boat"—both provide a wonderfully fresh crunch.

1. Pour 1 cup water into the Instant Pot. Place a trivet with handles in the pot. Carefully arrange the eggs on the trivet. Secure the lid on the pot and close the pressure-release valve. Set the pot to **HIGH** pressure for 5 minutes. At end of the cooking time, quick-release the pressure. Open the pot and gently place the eggs in a bowl of ice water for 10 minutes. Refrigerate for 30 minutes.

2. Peel the eggs, then chop into a medium dice and place in a medium bowl. Add the olives, feta, olive oil, lemon juice, oregano, dill, and pepper and stir to combine. Let sit 5 minutes for the flavors to develop. Season with pink salt and additional black pepper, if desired.

3. If using cucumber, halve the cucumber lengthwise and scoop out the centers, keeping about ¼ inch on the sides. Cut each cucumber half in half (you should have 4 total pieces). Divide the egg salad among the cucumber pieces. If using romaine, simply spread out the leaves and top with egg salad. Garnish with additional fresh dill, if desired.

Per serving: Calories: 259 • Total Fat: 19 g • Protein: 14 g • Total Carbs: 7 g • Fiber: 1 g • Erythritol: 0 g • Net Carbs: 6 g

10 INGREDIENTS OR LESS

Serves: 2
Active prep time: 15 minutes
Cook time: 5 minutes

4 large eggs
4 Kalamata olives, pitted and minced
1½ tablespoons crumbled feta cheese
1 tablespoon olive oil
1 tablespoon fresh lemon juice
¼ teaspoon dried oregano
⅛ teaspoon dried dill
¼ teaspoon black pepper
Fine Himalayan pink salt
1 English cucumber or 4 romaine lettuce leaves
Fresh dill, for serving (optional)

Double-Pork Egg Bites

Egg bites are one of my favorite quick keto breakfasts. You can make them in advance and stash them in the fridge or freezer so that you can reheat them in seconds and grab and go on your way to work or school. This version includes two of my favorite ingredients, pancetta and prosciutto, but you can use any leftover meat or veggies in egg bites. Don't bother with those fancy-looking egg bites at the coffee shop—these are way better and much more affordable!

Serves: 3
Active prep time: 10 minutes
Cook time: 8 minutes

1 tablespoon olive oil
¼ cup diced pancetta
¼ cup chopped prosciutto
Butter or ghee, for the egg bite mold
3 large eggs
½ cup diced seeded tomato
½ cup shredded mozzarella cheese (2 ounces)
¼ cup heavy cream
1 tablespoon prepared basil pesto
¼ teaspoon fine Himalayan pink salt
¼ teaspoon black pepper

1. Select **SAUTÉ** on the Instant Pot. When the pot is hot, add the olive oil. Add the pancetta and prosciutto to the hot oil and cook, stirring often, until the prosciutto gets crispy and some of the fat is rendered from the pancetta, about 3 minutes. Select **CANCEL**. Remove the meats from the pot and set aside.

2. Lightly grease 6 cups of a silicone egg bite mold with butter. Place on a trivet with handles. In a medium bowl, whisk together the eggs, tomato, mozzarella, cream, pesto, pink salt, and black pepper. Add the reserved meats. Pour the egg mixture into the 6 greased cups (about ¼ cup per cup).

3. Pour 1 cup water into the Instant Pot. Carefully lower the trivet and mold into the pot. Cover the mold with a paper towel and then foil.

4. Secure the lid on the pot and close the pressure-release valve. Set the pot to **LOW** pressure for 8 minutes. (If your electric pressure cooker doesn't have a low setting you can set your pot to **HIGH** pressure for 5 minutes.) At the end of the cooking time, use a natural release to depressurize for 5 minutes, then quick-release the remaining pressure.

5. Open the pot, remove the trivet, and let the egg bites cool for 2 minutes. Remove the bites from the mold using a spoon. Serve immediately or refrigerate for up to 3 days in a tightly covered container.

Per serving: Calories: 384 • Total Fat: 34 g • Protein: 19 g • Total Carbs: 3 g • Fiber: 0 g • Erythritol: 0 g • Net Carbs: 3 g

Lemon-Blueberry Pancake Cake with Fresh Thyme

Lemon and blueberry is one of my all-time favorite flavor combinations—it just tastes like summer, and the lemon really adds some extra zing to the berries. Here the addition of fragrant thyme elevates that combination even more. My daughter and I love making one massive pancake in the pressure cooker, and we always have leftovers for the next morning. Feel free to switch up the berries depending on what you have on hand (or what's on sale!).

1. In a small microwave-safe dish, microwave 3 tablespoons of the butter for 30 seconds or until melted. Transfer to a blender or food processor and add the eggs, cream cheese, ¼ cup of the coconut flour, the baking powder, the 1 teaspoon stevia, and the 1 teaspoon vanilla. Process or blend until smooth.

2. In a medium bowl, combine the blueberries, thyme, lemon zest, and the remaining 1 tablespoon coconut flour and toss to coat. Add the batter to the bowl and fold to combine.

3. Grease a 7-inch round baking dish with the remaining 1 tablespoon butter. Transfer the batter to the prepared dish. Coat a piece of foil with cooking spray and tightly cover the baking dish.

4. Pour 1 cup water into the Instant Pot. Place a trivet with handles in the pot and place the baking dish on the trivet. Secure the lid on the pot and close the pressure-release valve. Set the pot to **HIGH** pressure for 15 minutes. At the end of the cooking time, use a natural release to depressurize.

5. Meanwhile, make the whipped cream: In a medium bowl, with an electric mixer, beat together the cream and the ½ teaspoon stevia and ¼ teaspoon vanilla. Beat on medium-high until soft peaks form (tips curl).

6. Cut the pancake cake into 4 wedges. Serve with whipped cream. If desired, garnish with additional blueberries, lemon zest, and fresh thyme leaves.

Serves: 4
Active prep time: 15 minutes
Cook time: 15 minutes

4 tablespoons butter or ghee
4 large eggs
4 ounces cream cheese, cut into cubes
¼ cup plus 1 tablespoon coconut flour
1½ teaspoons baking powder
1 teaspoon liquid stevia
1 teaspoon vanilla extract
½ cup blueberries
2 teaspoons fresh thyme leaves
2 teaspoons grated lemon zest

For the whipped cream:
¼ cup heavy cream
½ teaspoon liquid stevia
¼ teaspoon vanilla extract

Per serving: Calories: 378 • Total Fat: 33 g • Protein: 10 g • Total Carbs: 11 g • Fiber: 4 g • Erythritol: 0 g • Net Carbs: 7 g

Pancake Bites

Combining salty bacon and pecans with keto-friendly maple syrup has to be one of the tastiest possible ways to start your day. You use a silicone egg bite mold to make these pancake bites, the same one you use to make egg bites—the result is small, pop-able pancakes loved by kids and adults alike. If you don't have pecans in your pantry you can always use chopped almonds or macadamia nuts instead.

10 INGREDIENTS OR LESS

Serves: 3
Active prep time: 10 minutes
Cook time: 8 minutes

Butter or ghee, for the egg bite mold
4 slices uncured bacon, chopped
2 tablespoons chopped pecans
4 large eggs
4 ounces cream cheese, at room temperature
3 tablespoons butter or ghee, melted
3 tablespoons coconut flour
1 tablespoon ChocZero maple syrup (or sugar-free syrup of your choice), plus more for serving
1½ teaspoons baking powder
⅛ teaspoon pumpkin pie spice

1. Coat 6 cups of a silicone egg bite mold with butter. Set aside.

2. Coat the inside of the Instant Pot with cooking spray. Select **SAUTÉ**. Add the bacon and pecans. Cook and stir until the bacon is crisp, 4 to 6 minutes. Select **CANCEL**. Divide the bacon and pecans among the greased egg bite cups.

3. In a blender or food processor, combine the eggs, cream cheese, melted butter, coconut flour, ChocZero, baking powder, and pumpkin pie spice. Blend or process until smooth. Divide the mixture among the egg bite cups. Cover the mold with foil.

4. Pour 1 cup water into the Instant Pot. Place a trivet with handles in the pot and place the egg mold on the trivet. Secure the lid on the pot and close the pressure-release valve. Set the pot to **STEAM** for 8 minutes. At the end of the cooking time, use a natural release to depressurize for 10 minutes, then quick-release the remaining pressure. Open the pot and gently lift the trivet and egg mold out. Invert the mold onto a wire rack.

5. Serve with additional sugar-free maple syrup.

Per serving: Calories: 506 • Total Fat: 43 g • Protein: 16 g • Total Carbs: 22 g • Fiber: 17 g • Erythritol: 0 g • Net Carbs: 5 g

Bacon-Cheddar Frittata with Tomato-Avocado Relish

Frittatas are a crowd pleaser in my family. Every time I go to my parents' house for holidays (they don't eat keto), they always ask me to make it. Frittatas are so easy to whip up, and I love being able to make a dish that everyone is excited to eat, regardless of their lifestyle. The classic team of bacon and cheddar makes this frittata wonderfully savory, while the relish adds freshness and a little heat. If you prefer, you can replace the bacon with 6 ounces of Italian sausage.

1. Make the frittata: Select **SAUTÉ** on the Instant Pot. When the pot is hot, add the bacon and cook, stirring often, until browned and crisp, 4 to 6 minutes. Select **CANCEL**. Transfer the bacon to paper towels to drain. Clean the pot and return to the Instant Pot.

2. In a medium bowl, whisk together the eggs, cheddar cheese, cream, pink salt, and black pepper. Stir in the reserved bacon. Generously brush a 6-inch round baking dish with olive oil or melted butter. Pour the egg mixture into the dish and cover tightly with foil.

3. Pour 1 cup water into the Instant Pot. Place a trivet with handles in the pot and place the dish on the trivet. Secure the lid on the pot and close the pressure-release valve. Set the pot to **HIGH** pressure for 12 minutes. At the end of the cooking time, use a natural release to depressurize for 15 minutes, then quick-release the remaining pressure.

4. Meanwhile, make the tomato-avocado relish: In a small bowl, combine the tomatoes, avocado, cilantro, green onions, jalapeño, lime juice, and cayenne. Season with pink salt and pepper, if desired.

5. Open the pot. Remove the trivet and baking dish and let the frittata cool in the dish for 2 minutes. Cut into wedges and serve with the tomato-avocado relish.

Per serving: Calories: 380 • Total Fat: 31 g • Protein: 19 g • Total Carbs: 8 g • Fiber: 3 g • Erythritol: 0 g • Net Carbs: 5 g

Serves: 4
Active prep time: 15 minutes
Cook time: 12 minutes

For the frittata:
4 slices uncured bacon, chopped
6 large eggs
¾ cup finely shredded cheddar cheese (3 ounces)
¼ cup grass-fed heavy cream
¼ teaspoon fine Himalayan pink salt
¼ teaspoon black pepper
Olive oil or melted butter, for the baking dish

For the tomato-avocado relish:
1 cup halved grape tomatoes
1 avocado, diced
¼ cup chopped fresh cilantro
2 green onions, finely chopped
1 jalapeño pepper, seeded and minced
1 tablespoon fresh lime juice
Pinch of cayenne pepper
Fine Himalayan pink salt and black pepper (optional)

Eggs and Bacon Avocado Boats

Avocados are the cornerstone of these "boats"—and they're also a cornerstone of the keto diet: They're full of heathy fats (both monounsaturated and polyunsaturated) and unlike many other fat sources, they're full of fiber. Plus they offer more potassium than a banana, so they're great for people struggling with the keto flu. For a dash of heat, I like to add a little sriracha or hot sauce to the top.

10 INGREDIENTS OR LESS

Serves: 4
Active prep time: 10 minutes
Cook time: 7 minutes

2 slices uncured bacon, finely chopped
4 large eggs
2 tablespoons heavy cream
2 tablespoons shredded Swiss cheese
1 tablespoon grass-fed butter, cut into cubes
1 tablespoon chopped fresh chives or dill
Pinch of fine Himalayan pink salt
Black pepper
2 avocados, halved and pitted
Sriracha (optional)

1. Select **SAUTÉ** on the Instant Pot. When the pot is hot, add the bacon. Cook until crisp, stirring occasionally, 4 to 6 minutes. Select **CANCEL**. Transfer the bacon to paper towels to drain. Clean the pot.

2. Coat a 7-inch round ceramic baking dish with cooking spray. Break the eggs into the dish and lightly beat with a fork or small whisk. Stir in the cream, adding the cheese, butter, chives, pink salt, and black pepper to taste.

3. Pour 1 cup water into the Instant Pot. Place a trivet with handles in the pot and place the dish on the trivet. Secure the lid on the pot and close the pressure-release valve. Set the pot to **LOW** pressure for 7 minutes (or **HIGH** for 4 minutes). At the end of the cooking time, quick-release the pressure. Let stand 1 minute in the pot. Carefully remove the dish and trivet from the pot.

4. Cut two avocados in half, placing one half on each of four plates. Divide the egg mixture among them. If desired, season with sriracha. Sprinkle with the bacon.

Per serving: Calories: 270 • Total Fat: 23 g • Protein: 10 g • Total Carbs: 7 g • Fiber: 5 g • Erythritol: 0 g • Net Carbs: 2 g

Sides

Cauliflower Jalapeño Popper

Do people exist who *don't* like jalapeño poppers?! If they do, I've never met them. Most poppers you'll find on restaurant menus or in the frozen section of your grocery store are covered with breading of some kind, but this keto-friendly version uses cauliflower to keep carbs in check. I've also added queso fresco to the party for a crazy delicious side dish or app guaranteed to win over any crowd.

1. Select **SAUTÉ** on the Instant Pot. When the pot is hot, add the bacon and cook, stirring often, until crisp, 4 to 6 minutes. Select **CANCEL**. Transfer the bacon to paper towels to drain. Pour out the bacon grease and discard.

2. In a bowl, combine the cream cheese, queso fresco, cauliflower, and jalapeño. Coat a 7-inch round baking dish with butter. Scrape the cauliflower mixture into the baking dish.

3. Pour 1 cup water into the Instant Pot. Place a trivet with handles in the pot and place the baking dish on the trivet. Secure the lid on the pot and close the pressure-release valve. Set the pot to **HIGH** pressure for 7 minutes. At the end of the cooking time, quick-release the pressure. Carefully remove the trivet and baking dish.

4. If desired, brown the top: Preheat the broiler to high. Broil 4 inches from the heat source until the top is lightly browned, 2 to 3 minutes.

5. Serve topped with the bacon.

Per serving: Calories: 327 · Total Fat: 28 g · Protein: 11 g · Total Carbs: 9 g · Fiber: 2 g · Erythritol: 0 g · Net Carbs: 7 g

10 INGREDIENTS OR LESS

Serves: 4
Active prep time: 10 minutes
Cook time: 7 minutes

4 slices uncured bacon, diced

8 ounces cream cheese, cut into cubes, at room temperature

½ cup shredded queso fresco (2 ounces)

4 cups roughly chopped cauliflower florets

2 jalapeño peppers, chopped (and seeded, if desired)

Butter or ghee, for the baking dish

Four-Cheese Cracked Pepper Broccoli

I never liked broccoli or cauliflower growing up, which is so crazy because now I eat tons of these super-healthy cruciferous veggies. Maybe my mom just didn't put enough cheese on them? If she'd made me this version, which uses four different kinds of cheese, I would have asked for seconds! This is a great go-to recipe for the vegetable-averse diners in your household.

Serves: 4
Active prep time: 5 minutes
Cook time: 1 minute

4 tablespoons butter or ghee
2 cloves garlic, minced
5 cups large broccoli florets
⅓ cup chicken broth
¼ cup heavy cream
2 ounces cream cheese, diced
½ cup shredded cheddar cheese (2 ounces)
¼ cup shredded Swiss cheese (1 ounce)
2 tablespoons grated Parmesan cheese
¾ to 1 teaspoon freshly cracked black pepper, to taste
Pinch of grated nutmeg

1. Select **SAUTÉ** on the Instant Pot. Add the butter. When the butter is melted, add the garlic and cook and stir for 1 minute. Select **CANCEL**. Stir in the broccoli and broth.

2. Secure the lid on the pot and close the pressure-release valve. Set the pot to **STEAM** for 1 minute. At the end of the cooking time, quick-release the pressure.

3. Select **SAUTÉ**. Add the cream and simmer for 2 minutes to slightly reduce. Select **CANCEL**. Gently stir in the cream cheese, cheddar, and Swiss cheese.

4. Serve sprinkled with the Parmesan, pepper, and nutmeg.

Per serving: Calories: 343 • Total Fat: 30 g • Protein: 11 g • Total Carbs: 10 g • Fiber: 3 g • Erythritol: 0 g • Net Carbs: 7 g

Bloody Mary Deviled Eggs

I am a deviled egg aficionado, which is a fancy way of saying I'm obsessed. I also enjoy a Bloody Mary from time to time, so why not combine those flavors in one perfect bite? These deviled eggs are a great side to serve at brunch or any other time of day. I think pickles are essential to a great deviled egg, but if for some crazy reason you aren't a pickle fan, you could substitute a tablespoon of diced celery or green olives. Feel free to get creative (have you seen the crazy toppings for Bloody Marys these days?!) and have fun!

1. Pour 1 cup water into the Instant Pot. Place a trivet with handles in the pot. Carefully arrange the eggs on the trivet. Secure the lid on the pot and close the pressure-release valve. Set the pot to **HIGH** pressure for 5 minutes. At the end of the cooking time, quick-release the pressure. Gently place the eggs in a bowl of ice water for 10 minutes. Refrigerate for 30 minutes.

2. Peel the eggs. Slice each egg in half lengthwise. Scoop out the egg yolks and place in a medium bowl. Place the egg whites on a serving platter and set aside.

3. To the egg yolks, add the mayonnaise, Worcestershire, tomato paste, dill pickle, and pickle juice. Mash with a fork to combine. Stir in the celery salt and cayenne.

4. Divide the filling among the egg whites. Garnish with the minced celery and a sprinkling of paprika.

Per serving: Calories: 143 • Total Fat: 12 g • Protein: 6 g • Total Carbs: 1 g • Fiber: 0 g • Erythritol: 0 g • Net Carbs: 1 g

10 INGREDIENTS OR LESS

Serves: 6
Active prep time: 15 minutes
Cook time: 5 minutes

6 large eggs
¼ cup avocado-oil mayonnaise
2 teaspoons Worcestershire sauce
1 teaspoon tomato paste
2 tablespoons minced dill pickle
2 teaspoons dill pickle juice
¼ teaspoon celery salt
⅛ teaspoon cayenne pepper
2 tablespoons minced celery
Sweet paprika, for garnish

Cajun Collard Greens and Pearl Onions

One of the benefits of cooking with a pressure cooker is that it infuses flavor into food quickly—and these Cajun collard greens are a perfect example. I love adding hot sauce and Cajun seasoning to mine, but you can also make Spanish-style collard greens by using ½ teaspoon smoked paprika and dried oregano instead (also omitting the hot pepper sauce). Either way, I'm sure these will soon become a part of your standard "sides" rotation!

10 INGREDIENTS OR LESS

Serves: 4
Active prep time: 10 minutes
Cook time: 20 minutes

5 slices uncured bacon, chopped
1 cup frozen pearl onions or ¾ cup chopped onions
2 bunches collard greens, washed and chopped (leaves and ribs)
1 cup chicken broth
1 teaspoon Cajun seasoning
¼ teaspoon garlic salt
2 tablespoons apple cider vinegar, distilled white vinegar, or lemon juice
Hot pepper sauce (optional)

1. Select SAUTÉ on the Instant Pot. When the pot is hot, add the bacon and cook, stirring occasionally, until just crisp, 4 to 6 minutes. Remove the bacon and set aside.

2. Carefully add the onions to the bacon drippings. Cook for 3 minutes, stirring occasionally. Return half of the bacon to the pot. Add the collard greens, broth, Cajun seasoning, and garlic salt and stir to combine. Select CANCEL.

3. Secure the lid on the pot and close the pressure-release valve. Set the pot to HIGH pressure for 20 minutes. At the end of the cooking time, quick-release the pressure.

4. Open the pot and stir in the vinegar and reserved bacon. If desired, season with hot pepper sauce.

Per serving: Calories: 231 · Total Fat: 19 g · Protein: 8 g · Total Carbs: 6 g · Fiber: 3 g · Erythritol: 0 g · Net Carbs: 3 g

Greek Cauliflower Rice

Cauliflower rice is a standby of the keto diet—it makes a perfect base or side for so many meals. I also love that it cooks perfectly and quickly in an Instant Pot. It doesn't have a ton of flavor on its own, so you can really use it as a blank canvas for all kinds of delicious combinations. Greek flavors are some of my favorites, and I almost always have the ingredients on hand, so this is a version that I make a lot. Chopped fresh herbs like dill, mint, and oregano are also great additions to this dish.

1. Pour 1 cup water into the Instant Pot. Place the cauliflower on a trivet with handles and lower the trivet into the pot. Secure the lid on the pot and close the pressure-release valve. Set the pot to **HIGH** pressure for 0 minutes (see Tip). At the end of the cooking time, quick-release the pressure. Transfer the cauliflower to a large bowl and set aside. Discard the liquid from the pot and wipe dry.

2. Select **SAUTÉ** on the Instant Pot. When the pot is hot, add 1 tablespoon of the olive oil. Add the onion and garlic to the hot oil and cook until tender, 3 to 4 minutes. Select **CANCEL**. Return the cauliflower to the pot and use a potato masher or wooden spoon to break the chunks into small, rice-size pieces.

3. Transfer the cauliflower to a serving bowl. Add the tomatoes, cucumber, olives, feta, parsley, lemon zest, and lemon juice and toss gently to combine. Sprinkle with the pink salt and pepper. Just before serving, fold in the walnuts and drizzle with the remaining 1 tablespoon olive oil.

Pressure Cooker Tip: Use the 0 minutes cook time for foods that don't need a lot of time to cook, like cauliflower florets. The pressure cooker will still build pressure, and as it does, it will cook the food—which will also continue to cook while the pressure is being released.

Serves: 8
Active prep time: 10 minutes
Cook time: 0 minutes

1 small head cauliflower, trimmed and cut into quarters
2 tablespoons olive oil
½ cup diced red onion
1 tablespoon minced garlic
1 cup halved grape tomatoes
½ cup chopped English cucumber
½ cup halved Kalamata olives
½ cup crumbled feta cheese
¼ cup chopped fresh parsley
Grated zest and juice of 1 lemon
¼ teaspoon fine Himalayan pink salt
¼ teaspoon black pepper
¼ cup chopped walnuts, toasted if desired

Per serving: Calories: 95 • Total Fat: 7 g • Protein: 3 g • Total Carbs: 6 g • Fiber: 2 g • Erythritol: 0 g • Net Carbs: 4 g

Cauliflower Fried Rice

I went through a phase where I ate fried rice constantly—something about the flavor and textures was just addicting. This keto-friendly version satisfies my cravings without tons of carbs. Bacon may not be a traditional ingredient, but I like to add a little for salt and protein. Of course, if you're looking for a meatless option, you can leave it out and add a wilted green like spinach.

Serves: 4
Active prep time: 15 minutes
Cook time: 0 minutes

1 small head cauliflower, trimmed and cut into florets
3 slices uncured bacon, diced
1 tablespoon toasted sesame oil
4 green onions, chopped
2 tablespoons minced fresh ginger
2 cloves garlic, minced
3 large eggs, lightly beaten
½ cup shredded carrot
½ cup frozen peas
1 tablespoon coconut aminos, tamari, or soy sauce
Toasted sesame seeds (optional)

1. Pour 1 cup water into the Instant Pot. Place a trivet with handles in the pot. Add the cauliflower. Secure the lid on the pot and close the pressure-release valve. Set the pot to **HIGH** pressure for 0 minutes (see Tip on page 65). At the end of the cooking time, quick-release the pressure. Remove the cauliflower and set it aside. Pour the cooking liquid out of the pot and wipe the pot dry.

2. Select **SAUTÉ** on the Instant Pot. Add the bacon and cook, stirring frequently, until browned and crisp, 4 to 6 minutes. Remove the bacon from the pot. Add the sesame oil to the bacon drippings in the pot. Add the green onions, ginger, and garlic and stir-fry until fragrant, about 1 minute. Return the cauliflower to the pot and use a potato masher or wooden spoon to break the chunks into small, rice-size pieces.

3. Move the cauliflower mixture to one side of the pot. Coat the empty portion with cooking spray. Add the eggs and cook, stirring constantly, until scrambled, about 1 minute. Add the carrot, peas, coconut aminos, and reserved bacon. Stir the cauliflower rice into the egg. Select **CANCEL**. Sprinkle with toasted sesame seeds before serving, if desired.

Per serving: Calories: 173 • Total Fat: 12 g • Protein: 8 g • Total Carbs: 7 g • Fiber: 2 g • Erythritol: 0 g • Net Carbs: 5 g

Creamed Brussels Sprouts with Bacon

My daughter will eat almost anything, but brussels sprouts have never been her favorite. This recipe, with lots of cheese and crispy pork rinds, has changed her mind completely. Watch out creamed spinach and creamed corn, there's a new side dish in town—and this one is here to stay.

1. Select **SAUTÉ** on the Instant Pot. Add the bacon and cook, stirring frequently, until browned and crisp, 4 to 6 minutes. Transfer the bacon to paper towels to drain.

2. Add the butter to the bacon drippings to melt. Add the brussels sprouts and seasoning mix. Sauté the sprouts, stirring occasionally, until lightly browned, 3 to 4 minutes. Add the cream, broth, and cream cheese. Select **CANCEL**.

3. Secure the lid on the pot and close the pressure-release valve. Set the pot to **HIGH** pressure for 1 minute. At the end of the cooking time, quick-release the pressure.

4. Stir the brussels sprouts. Sprinkle with the Parmesan, pepper, and bacon. Sprinkle crushed pork rinds on top of the sprouts before serving, if desired.

Per serving: Calories: 459 • Total Fat: 42 g • Protein: 11 g • Total Carbs: 13 g • Fiber: 4 g • Erythritol: 0 g • Net Carbs: 9 g

10 INGREDIENTS OR LESS

Serves: 4
Active prep time: 15 minutes
Cook time: 1 minute

3 slices uncured bacon, diced
3 tablespoons butter or ghee
1 pound brussels sprouts, trimmed and halved lengthwise
2 teaspoons Everything Bagel Seasoning
½ cup heavy cream
½ cup chicken broth
4 ounces cream cheese, cubed
2 tablespoons grated Parmesan cheese
½ teaspoon black pepper
Crushed pork rinds (optional)

Fiesta Cauliflower

Mexican flavors are some of my favorites, and luckily they tend to be keto-friendly. In this lively side, cilantro, lime juice, and jalapeños give regular old cauliflower rice a nice kick. I like to sprinkle a little Tajín chile-lime seasoning on top to give it some extra zing as well. If you prefer to make your own cauliflower rice, refer to the Greek Cauliflower Rice recipe on page 65.

Serves: 4

Active prep time: 15 minutes

Cook time: 4 minutes

- 4 mini sweet peppers, thinly sliced into rings
- 2 jalapeño peppers, seeded and diced
- ¼ cup diced red onion
- ¼ cup minced fresh cilantro
- 1 cup cubed pepper Jack cheese
- Grated zest of 1 lime
- 2 tablespoons fresh lime juice
- 1 teaspoon minced garlic
- ¼ cup avocado oil
- ½ teaspoon fine Himalayan pink salt
- ¼ teaspoon black pepper
- 1 (16-ounce) package frozen cauliflower rice

1. In a large bowl, combine all the ingredients except the cauliflower rice. Set aside.

2. Place the cauliflower rice in a 7-inch round baking dish. Pour 1 cup water into the Instant Pot. Place a trivet with handles in the pot and place the baking dish on the trivet. Secure the lid on the pot and close the pressure-release valve. Set the pot to STEAM for 4 minutes. At the end of the cooking time, quick-release the pressure.

3. Open the pot and transfer the hot cauliflower rice to the large bowl. Toss to combine.

Per serving: Calories: 263 • Total Fat: 22 g • Protein: 7 g • Total Carbs: 8 g • Fiber: 3 g • Erythritol: 0 g • Net Carbs: 5 g

Savory Greek Cheesy "Cake"

Have you ever tried a savory cheesecake? If not, let's make today the day! I like to serve this Greek-style cheese "cake" slightly chilled or at room temperature as a side for fish, chicken, or a main-dish salad. You can also serve it as an elegant appetizer spread on celery sticks.

1. In a food processor, pulse the almonds until finely ground. Add the butter and pulse just until combined. Press the nut mixture onto the bottom of a 6-inch springform pan. Place the pan on a full sheet of paper towel. Cut a piece of foil the size of the paper towel and place under the paper towel. Set aside.

2. Reserving 1 tablespoon of the marinade, drain the artichokes and cut half of the artichokes into quarters and keep the other half whole.

3. In a large bowl, with an electric mixer, beat the cream cheese for 30 seconds. Add the feta and beat well. Add the egg and beat just until blended. Stir in the quartered artichokes, the reserved marinade, and half of the green onions. Pour the mixture over the crust in the pan. Bring up the paper towel and foil around the pan. Cover the top of the pan with foil.

4. Pour 1 cup water into the Instant Pot. Place a trivet with handles in the pot and place the pan on the trivet.

5. Secure the lid on the pot and close the pressure-release valve. Set the pot to **HIGH** pressure for 35 minutes. At the end of the cooking time, use natural release to depressurize for 15 minutes, then quick-release the remaining pressure. Using the trivet handles, carefully remove the dish from the pot. Remove the foil and paper towel.

6. Cool the cheesecake on a wire rack for 1 hour. Cover and refrigerate for at least 4 hours or overnight.

7. To serve, loosen and remove the cheesecake from the sides of the pan. Top with the tomatoes, olives, and the remaining whole artichokes and green onions. Cut into wedges if serving as a side.

10 INGREDIENTS OR LESS

Serves: 6
Active prep time: 15 minutes
Cook time: 35 minutes

¾ cup toasted slivered almonds

2 tablespoons butter or ghee

1 (6-ounce) jar marinated artichokes, divided

12 ounces cream cheese, at room temperature

½ cup feta cheese crumbles with tomato and basil

1 large egg, at room temperature

¼ cup sliced green onions, divided

½ cup quartered grape tomatoes

2 tablespoons sliced pitted Kalamata olives

Per serving: Calories: 410 • Total Fat: 38 g • Protein: 9 g • Total Carbs: 9 g • Fiber: 2 g • Erythritol: 0 g • Net Carbs: 7 g

Spicy Bacon Green Bean Toss

I love green beans (always fresh, never out of a can!), and when I was growing up they were one of the few vegetables my mom liked, so she would make them all the time. This version is inspired by flavors that I use a lot with asparagus—turns out they are just as delicious with green beans.

10 INGREDIENTS OR LESS

Serves: 4
Active prep time: 10 minutes
Cook time: 1 minute

4 slices uncured bacon,
 chopped
1 small onion, finely chopped
1 pound green beans, trimmed
½ cup chicken broth
¼ cup grated Parmesan
 cheese
2 tablespoons butter or ghee
½ teaspoon crushed red
 pepper flakes

1. Select **SAUTÉ** on the Instant Pot. Add the bacon and cook, stirring occasionally, until crisp, 4 to 6 minutes. Transfer the bacon pieces to paper towels to drain. Add the onion to the bacon fat and cook, stirring often, until just tender, 2 to 3 minutes. Select **CANCEL**. Stir in the green beans and chicken broth.

2. Secure the lid on the pot and close the pressure-release valve. Set the pot to **LOW** pressure for 1 minute. At the end of the cooking time, quick-release the pressure.

3. Open the pot and select **SAUTÉ**. Simmer, stirring occasionally, until the liquid is reduced and the green beans are tender, 2 to 3 minutes. Select **CANCEL**. Stir in the Parmesan, butter, and pepper flakes. Sprinkle with the bacon just before serving.

Per serving: Calories: 180 • Total Fat: 13 g • Protein: 6 g • Total Carbs: 10 g • Fiber: 3 g • Erythritol: 0 g • Net Carbs: 7 g

Soups

Meat Lover's Chili

Chili is the ultimate comfort food; nothing tastes better or makes me feel cozier on a cold day. This three-meat chili comes together fast in the pressure cooker—no hours of simmering on the stove here—and makes for a perfect weeknight meal. One word of caution: I love the rich, smoky flavor of chipotle peppers, but they are very spicy. If you like your chili on the milder side, I recommend adding half a pepper; if you like it hot, go for two!

1. Select **SAUTÉ** on the Instant Pot. Add the bacon and cook, stirring, until crisp, 4 to 6 minutes. Drain. Crumble bacon and set aside. To the bacon fat, add the bell pepper, celery, and onion. Cook and stir until the vegetables are crisp-tender, about 4 minutes. Transfer to a medium bowl and set aside.

2. Melt the butter in the pot. Add the stew meat and cook, stirring occasionally, until browned, about 5 minutes. Transfer the meat to the bowl with the vegetables.

3. Add the ground beef and chorizo and cook, stirring occasionally, until the meat is browned, about 8 minutes. Return the veggies and stew meat to the pot. Stir in the broth, tomatoes, chili powder, and chipotle pepper(s). Select **CANCEL**.

4. Secure the lid on the pot and close the pressure-release valve. Set the pot to **HIGH** pressure for 35 minutes. At the end of the cooking time, use a natural release to depressurize.

5. Serve the chili topped with bacon, cheddar, and sour cream.

Per serving: Calories: 867 • Total Fat: 66 g • Protein: 54 g • Total Carbs: 11 g • Fiber: 2 g • Erythritol: 0 g • Net Carbs: 9 g

Serves: 4
Active prep time: 10 minutes
Cook time: 35 minutes

- 4 slices uncured bacon, chopped
- 1 green bell pepper, chopped
- 2 stalks celery, chopped
- ½ cup chopped onion
- 1 tablespoon butter or ghee
- 1 pound stew meat (such as chuck roast)
- ½ pound ground beef (80–85% lean)
- ½ pound fresh Mexican chorizo
- 3 cups beef broth
- 1 (14.5-ounce) can fire-roasted diced tomatoes
- 2 tablespoons chili powder
- 1 or 2 canned chipotle peppers in adobo sauce, to taste, minced
- ½ cup chopped fresh cilantro or sliced green onions
- 1 tablespoon shredded cheddar cheese, for serving
- 1 tablespoon sour cream, for serving

Chicken and Green Chile Soup

I fell in love with green chiles when I lived in Santa Fe, New Mexico, and cooking with them now always brings back memories of that beautiful state. This soup is another meal that comes together in just minutes using a pressure cooker, but you'd never know it from its deep, rich flavors. If you're dairy-free, you can omit the sour cream and instead add ½ cup canned coconut milk and ½ tablespoon fresh lemon juice—the consistency will be the same and the results are just as delicious!

Serves: 4
Active prep time: 15 minutes
Cook time: 15 minutes

1½ tablespoons olive oil
2 poblano peppers, seeded and diced
2 jalapeño peppers, seeded and diced
½ cup chopped white onion
2 cloves garlic, minced
2 cups chicken broth
½ teaspoon ground cumin
½ teaspoon dried oregano
½ teaspoon fine Himalayan pink salt
¼ teaspoon black pepper
1 pound bone-in chicken thighs, skin removed
½ cup sour cream
2 tablespoons chopped fresh cilantro, for serving
Lime wedges, for serving

1. Select **SAUTÉ** on the Instant Pot. When the pot is hot, add the olive oil. Add the poblanos, jalapeños, onion, and garlic to the hot oil and cook, stirring, until the vegetables are tender, 3 to 4 minutes. Select **CANCEL**.

2. Add the broth, 2 cups water, the cumin, oregano, pink salt, and black pepper to the pot. Stir to combine. Add the chicken. Secure the lid on the pot and close the pressure-release valve. Set the pot to **HIGH** pressure for 15 minutes. At the end of the cooking time, use a natural release to depressurize for 10 minutes, then quick-release the remaining pressure. Select **KEEP WARM**.

3. Carefully transfer the chicken to a cutting board. Use a fork to remove the chicken from the bone and shred it. Return the chicken to the pot (discard the bones).

4. Stir the sour cream into the pot until fully incorporated. Ladle into bowls and top each serving with cilantro and serve with lime wedges.

Per serving: Calories: 240 • Total Fat: 13 g • Protein: 20 g • Total Carbs: 9 g • Fiber: 1 g • Erythritol: 0 g • Net Carbs: 8 g

Italian Meatball Soup

It can be challenging to find keto versions of Italian food—after all, carbs are at the center of many Italian dishes—but this amazing meatball soup will make you feel like you're sitting at a cute little café in Tuscany. With the classic flavors of fresh garlic, Parmesan, and basil; a rich tomato broth; and tender, bite-size meatballs, this soup will satisfy all of your Italian cravings.

1. In a large bowl, combine the beef, onion, garlic, and egg, Parmesan, and Italian seasoning. Mix thoroughly, then shape the mixture into small meatballs (about 1 tablespoon each).

2. Select **SAUTÉ** on the Instant Pot. When hot, add 1 tablespoon of the olive oil. Add half the meatballs to the hot oil and sauté on all sides until browned (meatballs will not be cooked through), 3 to 4 minutes. Transfer the meatballs to a bowl. Repeat with the remaining 1 tablespoon olive oil and meatballs. Select **CANCEL**.

3. Return all the meatballs to the Instant Pot and add the broth and tomatoes. Secure the lid on the pot and close the pressure-release valve. Set the pot to **HIGH** pressure for 5 minutes. At the end of the cooking time, quick-release the pressure.

4. Add the spinach, basil, lemon zest, lemon juice, pink salt, and black pepper to the soup. Stir to wilt the spinach, sprinkle with reserved Parmesan, and serve.

Per serving: Calories: 342 • Total Fat: 21 g • Protein: 29 g • Total Carbs: 10 g • Fiber: 2 g • Erythritol: 0 g • Net Carbs: 8 g

Serves: 4
Active prep time: 15 minutes
Cook time: 12 minutes

1 pound ground beef (80–85% lean)
3 tablespoons grated onion
2 cloves garlic, minced
1 large egg
3 tablespoons grated Parmesan cheese, plus more for garnish
1 tablespoon Italian seasoning
2 tablespoons olive oil, divided
4 cups chicken broth
1 (14.5-ounce) can Italian-seasoned diced tomatoes in juice
1 (5-ounce) package fresh baby spinach
¼ cup chopped fresh basil leaves
Grated zest and juice of 1 lemon
⅓ teaspoon fine Himalayan pink salt
½ teaspoon black pepper

Coconut Milk Crab Bisque

Crab is my absolute favorite food—I could live off of a combination of crab legs and crab bisque for the rest of my life and be a very happy woman. Thankfully, I can eat as much of it as I like on keto. In my crab bisque I use coconut milk instead of cream—the result is a somewhat lighter bisque that I can enjoy more of without feeling too full! I highly recommend the wild-caught crabmeat in the frozen section at Trader Joe's—it's delicious and very affordable.

10 INGREDIENTS OR LESS

Serves: 2
Active prep time: 10 minutes
Cook time: 5 minutes

2 (6-ounce) cans lump
   crabmeat, undrained
1 cup sliced celery
1 cup quartered mushrooms
2 teaspoons tomato paste
1 cup vegetable broth
1 tablespoon butter or ghee
1½ teaspoons Old Bay
   seasoning
¼ teaspoon smoked paprika
1 cup coconut milk (or heavy
   cream if you prefer)
2 tablespoons chopped fresh
   celery leaves

1. In the Instant Pot, stir together the crabmeat with its liquid, celery, mushrooms, tomato paste, vegetable broth, butter, Old Bay, and smoked paprika. Secure the lid on the pot and close the pressure-release valve. Set the pot to **HIGH** pressure for 5 minutes. At the end of the cooking time, quick-release the pressure.

2. Open the pot and add the coconut milk. Use an immersion blender to blend until almost smooth. (Or, let the soup cool slightly and, working in batches, carefully transfer the soup to a blender, cover, and blend until almost smooth.)

3. Serve the soup hot, sprinkled with the celery leaves. I like to add a pinch of additional smoked paprika.

Per serving: Calories: 628 • Total Fat: 53 g • Protein: 33 g • Total Carbs: 9 g • Fiber: 2 g • Erythritol: 0 g • Net Carbs: 7 g

Pork Verde Soup

Tomatillos look like little green tomatoes surrounded by a papery husk (which you remove before using) and are typically available in the summer through the fall at farmers' markets. They have a distinctive taste—they're tart and have an herbal quality that pairs wonderfully with the Mexican flavors in this soup. I like to make little cheese crisps to eat with it, but note that the nutritional information does not include the crisps. You can make the crisps using any type of shredded cheese you like—my favorites are Mexican blend, asiago, or Parmesan.

1. Select **SAUTÉ** on the Instant Pot. When the pot is hot, add the coconut oil. Add the pork and onion to the hot oil and cook until browned, about 8 minutes. Add the broth, tomatillos, poblanos, salsa verde, 2 tablespoons of the cilantro, and the cumin. Select **CANCEL**.

2. Secure the lid on the pot and close the pressure-relief valve. Set the pot to **HIGH** pressure for 15 minutes. At the end of the cooking time, use a natural release to depressurize.

3. Open the pot and stir in the lime juice. Top each serving with the remaining 2 tablespoons cilantro and the avocado. If desired, serve with cheese crisps.

4. To make the cheese crisps: Preheat the oven to 375°F. Line a baking sheet with parchment paper. Create mounds of shredded cheese, using about 2 tablespoons of cheese per crisp, leaving room so they can spread as they cook. Bake until melted and golden around the edges, about 7 minutes. Let sit on the baking sheet until firm, then transfer to a wire rack or a plate lined with paper towels to cool for at least 10 minutes (they will crisp up the longer they sit).

Per serving: Calories: 255 • Total Fat: 9 g • Protein: 29 g • Total Carbs: 14 g • Fiber: 4 g • Erythritol: 0 g • Net Carbs: 10 g

Serves: 6
Active prep time: 15 minutes
Cook time: 15 minutes

2 teaspoons coconut oil or olive oil
1½ pounds boneless pork sirloin roast or shoulder roast, trimmed and cut into ½-inch chunks
½ cup chopped onion
2½ cups beef or chicken broth
1 pound fresh tomatillos, husked and quartered, or 1 (11-ounce) can tomatillos, drained and quartered
2 fresh poblano peppers, seeded and chopped, or 2 (4.5-ounce) cans diced green chiles
½ cup salsa verde
4 tablespoons chopped fresh cilantro, divided
2 teaspoons ground cumin
2 tablespoons fresh lime juice
1 avocado, coarsely chopped, for serving
Cheese crisps (optional)

For the cheese crisps:
1 cup shredded cheese

Lasagna Soup

I haven't had traditional carb-filled lasagna in years, but this soup gives me all of the same flavors and the cheese I love. I use thinly sliced zucchini to replace the lasagna noodles—you can use a mandoline set on the ¼-inch setting or a "Y" vegetable peeler to achieve a pasta-like thickness and shape. I like to finish off this soup with a few shakes of crushed red pepper flakes to add a little bit of heat!

10 INGREDIENTS OR LESS

Serves: 6
Active prep time: 15 minutes
Cook time: 3 minutes

1 pound bulk Italian sausage
½ cup chopped onion
4 cups chicken broth
1 medium zucchini, trimmed
   and sliced into wide
   lengthwise ribbons (see note
   above)
1 (14.5-ounce) can Italian
   stewed tomatoes
3 cloves garlic, minced
2 teaspoons Italian seasoning
¼ cup grated Parmesan
   cheese, for serving
¼ cup thinly sliced fresh basil,
   for serving
Crushed red pepper flakes, for
   serving (optional)

1. Select **SAUTÉ** on the Instant Pot. When the pot is hot, add the sausage and onion and cook, stirring occasionally, until the onion is tender and the sausage is no longer pink, about 8 minutes. Select **CANCEL.** Drain off any fat. Add the broth, zucchini, tomatoes, garlic, and Italian seasoning.

2. Secure the lid on the pot and close the pressure-release valve. Set the pot to **HIGH** pressure for 3 minutes. At the end of the cooking time, quick-release the pressure.

3. Ladle the soup into shallow bowls and top each serving with Parmesan, basil, and red pepper flakes, if desired.

Per serving: Calories: 270 • Total Fat: 18 g • Protein: 14 g • Total Carbs: 9 g • Fiber: 1 g • Erythritol: 0 g • Net Carbs: 8 g

Chicken Low-Carb Tortilla Soup

This soup is inspired by the flavors of classic chicken tortilla soup. It's one of my go-to recipes when I just want a simple, satisfying meal. It took all day to make in my slow cooker, but in the pressure cooker the whole process takes less than 30 minutes. If you're tired of chicken, you can swap in 2 pounds boneless pork butt, fat trimmed and cut into 3-inch pieces.

1. In the Instant Pot, stir together the jalapeños, tomatoes, broth, 3 cups water, cumin, oregano, garlic powder, pink salt, and black pepper. Add the chicken breasts.

2. Secure the lid on the pot and close the pressure-release valve. Set the pot to **HIGH** pressure for 15 minutes. At the end of the cooking time, use a natural release to depressurize for 10 minutes, then quick-release the remaining pressure.

3. Open the pot and carefully transfer the chicken to a cutting board. Pull the chicken meat off the bones and shred with two forks (discard the bones).

4. Return the shredded chicken to the pot and select **SAUTÉ**. Add the cream cheese and cheddar and cook, stirring constantly, until the cheeses are melted, about 5 minutes.

5. Serve the soup topped with the chopped cilantro and jalapeño slices, and optional tortilla strips.

Per serving: Calories: 498 • Total Fat: 32 g • Protein: 41 g • Total Carbs: 12 g • Fiber: 3 g • Erythritol: 0 g • Net Carbs: 9 g

Serves: 4
Active prep time: 10 minutes
Cook time: 15 minutes

2 jalapeño peppers, seeded and chopped, plus slices for garnish
1 (14.5-ounce) can diced tomatoes
1 cup chicken broth
½ teaspoon ground cumin
½ teaspoon dried oregano
½ teaspoon garlic powder
¼ teaspoon fine Himalayan pink salt
¼ teaspoon black pepper
2 bone-in chicken breasts, skin removed (about 1½ pounds)
4 ounces cream cheese, cut into ½-inch cubes
2 cups shredded mild cheddar cheese
2 tablespoons chopped fresh cilantro, for serving
Jalapeño slices, for serving (optional)
Tortilla strips, for serving (optional)

Creamy Tomato-Basil Soup

There is something so homey about tomato soup. It reminds me of snow days when I was a kid—though of course back then my bowl of soup was always paired with a grilled cheese. You can bring those same flavors together here by combining this creamy soup with my Cheese Crisps (page 87) or a sprinkle of the shredded cheese of your choice. Throw on your favorite sweater and dig in!

Serves: 6
Active prep time: 15 minutes
Cook time: 5 minutes

2 tablespoons butter or ghee
½ cup diced onion
½ cup diced celery
1 tablespoon Italian seasoning
2 cloves garlic, minced
1 (28-ounce) can Italian-
   seasoned diced tomatoes in
   juice
½ cup heavy cream or coconut
   cream
¼ cup thinly sliced fresh basil
½ teaspoon fine Himalayan
   pink salt
¼ teaspoon black pepper
Cheese Crisps (page 87) or
   shredded cheese (optional)

1. Select **SAUTÉ** on the Instant Pot. Add the butter, and when it has melted, add the onion, celery, Italian seasoning, and garlic. Cook, stirring frequently, until the vegetables are crisp-tender, about 5 minutes. Select **CANCEL**. Add the tomatoes and 3 cups water.

2. Secure the lid on the pot and close the pressure-release valve. Set the pot to **HIGH** pressure for 5 minutes. At the end of the cooking time, use a natural release to depressurize for 10 minutes, then quick-release the remaining pressure.

3. Use an immersion blender to blend the soup. (Or, let the soup cool slightly and, working in batches, carefully transfer the soup to a blender, cover, and blend until smooth. Return the soup to the pot.) Stir in the cream, basil, pink salt, and pepper.

4. Top with cheese crisps or shredded cheese, if desired, and serve.

Per serving: Calories: 144 • Total Fat: 11 g • Protein: 2 g •
Total Carbs: 9 g • Fiber: 2 g • Erythritol: 0 g • Net Carbs: 7 g

Sausage-Kale Soup

This is really a choose-your-own-adventure kind of recipe—you can use any type of sausage you prefer (kielbasa, chorizo, and Italian sausage are all great choices!), and depending on what you choose, you can really change the flavor profile of the soup. Likewise, you can add in any leafy green—spinach or chard would work well here if you're not on the kale bandwagon. Don't skip the cauliflower, though—it gives the soup a great bite and makes it very filling.

1. Select **SAUTÉ** on the Instant Pot. When the pot is hot, add the olive oil. Add the sausage, onion, garlic, paprika, and pepper flakes to the hot oil and cook, stirring often, until the onion softens and the sausage starts to brown, about 5 minutes. Select **CANCEL**. Add the broth and cauliflower rice.

2. Secure the lid on the pot and close the pressure-release valve. Set the pot to **HIGH** pressure for 5 minutes. At the end of the cooking time, quick-release the pressure.

3. Stir in the kale, pink salt, and pepper. Let the soup stand 5 minutes to soften the kale before serving.

Per serving: Calories: 310 • Total Fat: 24 g • Protein: 14 g • Total Carbs: 10 g • Fiber: 3 g • Erythritol: 0 g • Net Carbs: 7 g

Serves: 4
Active prep time: 10 minutes
Cook time: 5 minutes

2 tablespoons olive oil
½ pound uncured sausage, sliced into ½-inch-thick rounds
½ cup diced yellow onion
2 tablespoons minced garlic
½ teaspoon smoked paprika
¼ to ½ teaspoon crushed red pepper flakes, to taste
4 cups chicken broth
2 cups cauliflower rice
3 cups chopped fresh kale
¼ teaspoon fine Himalayan pink salt
¼ teaspoon black pepper

Buffalo Chicken Chowder

There are so many delicious carb-heavy dishes that begin with the words "Buffalo chicken"—from pizza to appetizers to salads topped with breaded chicken. This chowder delivers all of the classic flavor of Buffalo chicken without the carbs. Creamy, spicy, and instantly craveable, this soup will warm you up from head to toe.

10 INGREDIENTS OR LESS

Serves: 4
Active prep time: 25 minutes
Cook time: 15 minutes

4 tablespoons butter or ghee
½ cup chopped yellow onion
2 stalks celery, chopped (reserve some leaves for garnish)
2 cloves garlic, minced
2⅔ cups chicken broth
1½ pounds boneless, skinless chicken thighs
½ cup Buffalo-style hot sauce, plus more to taste
1⅓ cups heavy cream or coconut cream
3 tablespoons almond flour

1. Select **SAUTÉ** on the Instant Pot. Add 3 tablespoons of the butter. When the butter is melted, add the onion, celery, and garlic and cook, stirring occasionally, until just softened, 3 to 4 minutes. Select **CANCEL**. Stir in the chicken broth, chicken, and hot sauce.

2. Secure the lid on the pot and close the pressure-release valve. Set the pot to **HIGH** pressure for 15 minutes. At the end of the cooking time, quick-release the pressure.

3. Open the pot and remove the chicken. Shred the chicken into bite-size pieces and return to the pot. Select **SAUTÉ**. Stir in the cream and almond flour. Cook until the soup is thickened. Stir in the remaining 1 tablespoon butter and additional hot sauce to taste.

4. Serve sprinkled with the reserved celery leaves.

Per serving: Calories: 626 • Total Fat: 50 g • Protein: 38 g • Total Carbs: 6 g • Fiber: 1 g • Erythritol: 0 g • Net Carbs: 5 g

Chapter 7

Seafood

Coconut Curry Mussels with Zucchini Noodles

I love these mussels almost as much as I love the flavorful coconut-curry cooking liquid they're nestled in. Zucchini noodles soak up the bright flavors of the sauce and make this dish nice and filling. I purchase zucchini noodles prezoodled to save a little time, but if you have a spiralizer you can also do it yourself.

1. Select **SAUTÉ** on the Instant Pot. When the pot is hot, add 1 tablespoon of the avocado oil. Add the zucchini noodles to the hot oil and cook, stirring frequently, until just tender, 3 to 4 minutes. Select **CANCEL**. Transfer the zoodles to a dish and cover to keep warm.

2. Select **SAUTÉ** again. Add the remaining 2 tablespoons avocado oil to the pot. When the oil is hot, add the onion, ginger, garlic, and curry paste. Cook, stirring frequently, until fragrant, about 1 minute. Select **CANCEL**. Add the coconut milk, broth, mussels, and bell pepper to the pot.

3. Secure the lid and close the pressure-release valve. Set the pot to **HIGH** pressure for 3 minutes. At the end of the cooking time, quick-release the pressure. Discard any mussels that have not opened.

4. Divide the zucchini noodles and mussels among four shallow serving bowls. Stir the fish sauce, pink salt, pepper, and lime juice into the curry sauce, then pour over the mussels. Sprinkle with cilantro before serving.

Per serving: Calories: 269 • Total Fat: 20 g • Protein: 10 g • Total Carbs: 11 g • Fiber: 2 g • Erythritol: 0 g • Net Carbs: 9 g

Serves: 4
Active prep time: 15 minutes
Cook time: 8 minutes

3 tablespoons avocado oil
1 (10- to 12-ounce) package zucchini noodles or 2 large zucchini, zoodled
⅓ cup diced onion
2 tablespoons minced fresh ginger
4 cloves garlic, minced
1 tablespoon red curry paste
1 cup coconut milk
1 cup chicken broth
¾ pound (15 to 18) mussels, scrubbed, beards removed
½ medium red bell pepper, cut into strips
1 tablespoon fish sauce
½ teaspoon fine Himalayan pink salt
¼ teaspoon black pepper
Juice of ½ lime
¼ cup chopped fresh cilantro, for serving

Lemongrass-Steamed Crab Legs with Ginger-Garlic Ghee

I love to work for my food. Give me a couple hours and a giant plate of crab legs and I will happily put in the elbow grease to get every last bite of that deliciously sweet, delicate meat. Crab doesn't need much accompaniment, and plain old melted butter does the job just fine—but sometimes it's fun to play with flavors, especially in the pressure cooker because it can infuse flavor so quickly. I love the unique taste and scent of lemongrass, but if you can't find it at your market, feel free to swap in lemon zest, which will still pair nicely with the ginger and garlic.

10 INGREDIENTS OR LESS

Serves: 2
Active prep time: 10 minutes
Cook time: 3 minutes

2 pounds snow crab legs
½ cup sliced lemongrass or
   6 to 8 strips lemon zest
¼ cup sliced fresh ginger, plus
   1 tablespoon minced
2 teaspoons black
   peppercorns

For the butter dipping sauce:
8 tablespoons butter or ghee
2 cloves garlic, minced
1 tablespoon minced garlic
1 tablespoon sliced chives

1. Pour 1 cup water into the Instant Pot. Place a trivet with handles in the pot. Arrange the crab legs on the trivet. Sprinkle with the lemongrass, the sliced ginger, and peppercorns.

2. Secure the lid on the pot and close the pressure-release valve. Set the pot to **HIGH** pressure for 3 minutes. At the end of the cooking time, quick-release the pressure.

3. Meanwhile, make the butter dipping sauce: In a small microwave-safe container, combine the butter, garlic, minced ginger, and chives. Microwave for 1 minute or until the butter is melted.

4. Serve the crab legs with the butter for dipping.

Per serving: Calories: 719 • Total Fat: 61 g • Protein: 32 g • Total Carbs: 8 g • Fiber: 0 g • Erythritol: 0 g • Net Carbs: 8 g

Fish "Taco" Bowls

Eating fish tacos always makes me feel like I'm at the beach on vacation. At many restaurants (or, here in California, taco trucks), the fish is deep-fried to get a crispy texture. My version keeps things lighter and relies on shredded cabbage for texture and crunch. I like to layer with cauliflower rice on the bottom of the bowl, then pile on the cabbage, add the fish, avocado, and toppings. Full of fresh flavors and textures, these fish taco–inspired bowls are a great option for lunch or dinner.

1. In a small bowl, stir together the sour cream, lime juice, ¼ teaspoon of the pink salt, and the cilantro. Add the cabbage and toss to combine. Set aside.

2. Place the cauliflower rice in a microwave-safe bowl and cover with plastic wrap. Microwave for 3 minutes. Uncover, add 2 teaspoons of the avocado oil, the pepper, and the remaining ¼ teaspoon pink salt. Stir and cover to keep warm.

3. Drizzle the fish with the remaining 1 teaspoon avocado oil and rub taco seasoning on both sides. Pour 1 cup water into the Instant Pot. Place a trivet with handles in the pot. Place the fish on the trivet.

4. Secure the lid on the pot and close the pressure-release valve. Set the pot to **HIGH** pressure for 2 minutes. At the end of the cooking time, quick-release the pressure. Transfer the fish to a plate.

5. Divide the cauliflower and cabbage between two shallow bowls. Top with the fish and sliced avocado, and sprinkle with cilantro.

Serves: 2
Active prep time: 10 minutes
Cook time: 2 minutes

¼ cup sour cream
1 tablespoon fresh lime juice
¼ teaspoon fine Himalayan pink salt
1 tablespoon chopped fresh cilantro, plus more for garnish
1 cup packed shredded green or red cabbage
2 cups cauliflower rice
3 teaspoons avocado oil, divided
¼ teaspoon black pepper
1 teaspoon taco seasoning
2 red snapper fillets (6 ounces each)
1 avocado, sliced

Pressure Cooker Tip: The Instant Pot is the perfect tool for preparing fish! Try adding a few sprigs of any fresh herb you'd like to the water before cooking—its flavor will be subtly infused into the fish as it cooks.

Per serving: Calories: 426 • Total Fat: 24 g • Protein: 39 g • Total Carbs: 15 g • Fiber: 8 g • Erythritol: 0 g • Net Carbs: 7 g

Braised Salmon with Lemon and Olives

I probably eat salmon in one form or another four to five days a week. It's a perfect keto food because it's not only a good source of protein, it's also full of heart-healthy fats. Lemon is a classic pairing with salmon, but in this dish I've created more of a Mediterranean flavor profile with salty Kalamata olives, feta, and oregano. It is a perfect weeknight dinner that cooks in minutes and will leave your family asking for seconds.

Serves: 2
Active prep time: 15 minutes
Cook time: 3 minutes

1 tablespoon olive oil
1 small green bell pepper
2 cloves garlic, sliced
2 Roma (plum) tomatoes, chopped
1 bay leaf
1 teaspoon dried oregano
½ teaspoon crushed red pepper flakes
2 skin-on salmon fillets (6 ounces each)
½ teaspoon fine Himalayan pink salt
¼ teaspoon black pepper
1 tablespoon butter or ghee
¼ cup Kalamata olives, sliced
1 teaspoon grated lemon zest
2 teaspoons fresh lemon juice
¼ cup crumbled feta cheese

1. Select **SAUTÉ** on the Instant Pot. When the pot is hot, add the olive oil. Add the bell pepper and garlic to the hot oil and cook, stirring, until the pepper is softened, 2 to 3 minutes. Stir in the tomatoes, bay leaf, oregano, and pepper flakes. Season the salmon with the pink salt and black pepper. Set the salmon on top of the mixture in the pot. Select **CANCEL**.

2. Secure the lid on the pot and close the pressure-release valve. Set the pot to **HIGH** pressure for 3 minutes. At the end of the cooking time, quick-release the pressure.

3. Open the pot and carefully remove the salmon fillets. Stir the butter, olives, lemon zest, and lemon juice into the sauce. Serve the salmon with the sauce and sprinkle with the feta.

Per serving: Calories: 481 • Total Fat: 32 g • Protein: 38 • Total Carbs: 11 g • Fiber: 3 g • Erythritol: 0 g • Net Carbs: 8 g

Mediterranean Fish Bake

This fish bake is ultraflexible: you can substitute any mild white fish, such as tilapia, for the cod, or even salmon fillets if you aren't a fan of white fish. Layering the fish with aromatics much like you would if you were cooking en papillote or on the grill infuses a ton of flavor into the delicate meat, but in a fraction of the cooking time. Serve with Greek Cauliflower Rice (page 65) or Four-Cheese Cracked Pepper Broccoli (page 58) for a complete meal.

1. Drizzle the fish with some of the olive oil and sprinkle the Italian seasoning on both sides.

2. Select **SAUTÉ** on the Instant Pot. When the pot is hot, add the remaining oil. Add the onion and garlic to the hot oil and cook, stirring frequently, until the onion is tender, 2 to 3 minutes. Add the artichoke hearts and olives. Select **CANCEL**. Top with the fish in a single layer. Layer the lemon slices over the fish.

3. Secure the lid on the pot and close the pressure-release valve. Set the pot to **HIGH** pressure for 1 minute. At the end of the cooking time, quick-release the pressure.

4. Serve topped with the feta and basil.

Per serving: Calories: 286 · Total Fat: 11 g · Protein: 33 g · Total Carbs: 14 g · Fiber: 4 g · Erythritol: 0 g · Net Carbs: 10 g

10 INGREDIENTS OR LESS

Serves: 2
Active prep time: 10 minutes
Cook time: 1 minute

2 cod fillets (6 ounces each)
1 tablespoon olive oil ·
1 teaspoon Italian seasoning
⅓ cup thinly sliced onion
2 cloves garlic, minced
⅔ cup drained chopped artichoke hearts (about half a 13.75-ounce can)
4 to 6 pitted Kalamata olives, sliced
4 thin slices lemon
2 tablespoons crumbled feta cheese
1 tablespoon chopped fresh basil

Shrimp Italiano

Imagine seasoned shrimp swimming in a rich, creamy sauce with salty prosciutto. It's a meal I make often! The dish comes together quickly but feels very impressive (your dinner guests don't have to know it took you only ten minutes to prepare!). I usually throw the shrimp in the marinade earlier in the day so that once it's time to eat they're ready to go. If you want to add some more veggies to the mix, you can serve the shrimp over lightly sautéed zucchini noodles or summer squash noodles.

Serves: 4
Active prep time: 40 minutes
Cook time: 0 minutes

1 pound peeled and deveined
   large shrimp (about
   8 shrimp)
4 tablespoons olive oil, divided
4 cloves garlic, minced
Juice of 1 lemon
½ teaspoon crushed red
   pepper flakes
½ cup chopped prosciutto
½ cup diced yellow onion
1 tablespoon Italian seasoning
1 cup grape tomatoes
½ cup chicken broth
½ cup cream cheese, cubed
½ cup heavy cream
¼ teaspoon fine Himalayan
   pink salt
¼ teaspoon black pepper
½ cup thinly sliced fresh basil
   leaves, for garnish

1. In a resealable plastic bag, combine the shrimp, 3 tablespoons of the olive oil, the garlic, lemon juice, and pepper flakes. Shake gently to mix and coat the shrimp. Let the shrimp marinate for only 30 minutes. If you wish to marinate longer than 30 minutes, place in the refrigerator so the lemon juice doesn't "cook" the shrimp.

2. When ready to cook, select SAUTÉ on the Instant Pot. When the pot is hot, add the remaining 1 tablespoon olive oil. Add the prosciutto, onion, and Italian seasoning to the hot oil and cook, stirring frequently, until the onion softens, about 5 minutes. Add the tomatoes, broth, and shrimp with its marinade. Hit CANCEL.

3. Secure the lid on the pot and close the pressure-release valve. Set the pot to HIGH pressure for 0 minutes (see Tip on page 65). At the end of the cooking time, quick-release the pressure.

4. Open the pot and stir in the cream cheese, heavy cream, pink salt, and pepper until the cream cheese is melted. Serve sprinkled with basil.

Per serving: Calories: 484 • Total Fat: 39 g • Protein: 25 g • Total Carbs: 10 g • Fiber: 1 g • Erythritol: 0 g • Net Carbs: 9 g

Tuna Melt Egg Cups

I know it's probably not cool to admit this, but sometimes I crave a good tuna melt—there's something about that seemingly weird flavor combination that just works. My version ditches the bread in favor of protein-rich eggs, and I fold in some fresh herbs to brighten it all up. I like to use white cheddar for my "tuna melt" because it has so much flavor, but you could use any good melting cheese, like pepper Jack, Gouda, or provolone.

1. Select **SAUTÉ** on the Instant Pot. Add the bacon and cook, stirring occasionally, until crisp, 4 to 6 minutes. Select **CANCEL**. Transfer the bacon to paper towels to drain. Pour off the bacon fat and wipe out the pot.

2. In a medium bowl, whisk together the eggs and cream. Stir in the bacon, tuna, cheddar, dill, and chives.

3. Brush seven cups of a silicone egg bite mold with the melted better. Spoon the egg mixture into the cups. Add 1 cup water to the Instant Pot. Place a trivet with handles in the pot. Cover the egg bite mold with a piece of paper towel and then foil. Place the egg bite mold on the trivet.

4. Secure the lid on the pot and close the pressure-release valve. Set the pot to **HIGH** pressure for 8 minutes. At the end of the cooking time, use a natural release to depressurize for 5 minutes, then quick-release the remaining pressure.

5. Carefully remove the trivet and egg mold. Serve warm or at room temperature with sriracha, if desired.

10 INGREDIENTS OR LESS

Serves: 2
Active prep time: 10 minutes
Cook time: 8 minutes

4 slices uncured bacon, diced
4 large eggs
¼ cup heavy cream
1 (5-ounce) can tuna in olive oil, drained
¾ cup shredded white cheddar cheese (3 ounces)
1 tablespoon chopped fresh dill
2 teaspoons chopped fresh chives
1 tablespoon butter or ghee, melted
Sriracha (optional)

Per serving: Calories: 679 · Total Fat: 51 g · Protein: 49 g · Total Carbs: 3 g · Fiber: 0 g · Erythritol: 0 g · Net Carbs: 3 g

Lemon-Garlic Salmon

Here's another play on classic Mediterranean flavors, this one swapping in capers for olives. I love the awesome pop of briny flavor that capers add to any dish, and they pair perfectly with lemon juice and garlic to create a bright complement to the asparagus and salmon. This simple dish contains only 3 net carbs per serving and almost equal parts protein and fat, making it a great choice when you're in the early days of keto and trying to get fat-adapted or if you've accidentally slipped out of ketosis and are looking to get back on track.

10 INGREDIENTS OR LESS

Serves: 2
Active prep time: 10 minutes
Cook time: 3 minutes

1 tablespoon fresh lemon juice
¼ cup chopped fresh parsley
2 tablespoons avocado oil
2 cloves garlic, minced
2 teaspoons capers
¼ teaspoon fine Himalayan pink salt
¼ teaspoon black pepper
2 skin-on salmon fillets (4 to 6 ounces each)
8 thick spears asparagus, trimmed

1. In a small bowl, stir together the lemon juice, parsley, avocado oil, garlic, capers, pink salt, and pepper. Rub half of the parsley mixture on the salmon.

2. Pour 1 cup water into the Instant Pot. Place a trivet with handles in the pot. Place the asparagus on the trivet and top with the salmon, skin-side down.

3. Secure the lid on the pot and close the pressure-release valve. Set the pot to **HIGH** pressure for 3 minutes. At the end of the cooking time, quick-release the pressure.

4. Open the pot and carefully remove the trivet. Transfer the salmon and asparagus to two serving plates. Top the asparagus with the remaining parsley mixture.

Per serving: Calories: 304 • Total Fat: 21 g • Protein: 24 g • Total Carbs: 5 g • Fiber: 2 g • Erythritol: 0 g • Net Carbs: 3 g

Weeknight Shrimp Gumbo

Traditional Cajun gumbo takes hours or even days to prepare as it simmers on the stovetop and develops layers of flavor. There's nothing that can quite replicate that kind of flavor depth, but most of us don't have all day to cook a meal for our families—and that's where the pressure cooker comes into play. This dish is rich in bold flavors and takes less than 15 minutes to cook. Serve over cauliflower rice for an even more filling meal.

1. Select **SAUTÉ** on the Instant Pot. When the pot is hot, add the oil and coconut flour. Cook, stirring constantly until the roux is deeply golden, about 2 minutes. Carefully whisk in the broth. Add the tomatoes, sausage, okra, bell pepper, onion, celery, and Cajun seasoning. Select **CANCEL**.

2. Secure the lid on the pot and close the pressure-release valve. Set the pot to **HIGH** pressure for 8 minutes. At the end of the cooking time, use a natural release to depressurize.

3. Open the pot and select **SAUTÉ**. Stir in the shrimp and cook until the shrimp are pink and opaque, 2 to 3 minutes. Select **CANCEL**.

4. Serve the gumbo. If desired, pass hot sauce at the table.

Per serving: Calories: 354 · Total Fat: 27 g · Protein: 14 g · Total Carbs: 14 g · Fiber: 4 g · Erythritol: 0 g · Net Carbs: 10 g

Serves: 6
Active prep time: 15 minutes
Cook time: 8 minutes

¼ cup coconut oil or avocado oil
¼ cup coconut flour
2 cups chicken broth
1 (14.5-ounce) can fire-roasted diced tomatoes with garlic
12 ounces andouille sausage links sliced ½ inch thick
Half a 12-ounce package frozen cut okra, thawed
¼ cup chopped green bell pepper
¼ cup chopped onion
½ cup chopped celery
2 teaspoons Cajun seasoning or Old Bay seasoning
½ pound peeled and deveined medium shrimp (41/50 count)
Hot pepper sauce (optional), for serving

Coconut Green Curry Shrimp

Green curry paste is an ingredient I hadn't used much until recently, but now I'm obsessed with it. Made of chiles, garlic, basil, shallots, lemongrass, and ginger, it packs amazing flavor. This incredible-smelling shrimp dish tastes like something you'd order off a restaurant menu—it is that good. I like to top my bowl with chopped green onions, fresh herbs such as mint, basil, or cilantro, and a dash of sriracha.

10 INGREDIENTS OR LESS

Serves: 2
Active prep time: 5 minutes
Cook time: 7 minutes

Half a 14.5-ounce can coconut milk
1 tablespoon Thai green curry paste
2 teaspoons grated fresh ginger
2 cloves garlic, minced
¼ teaspoon fine Himalayan pink salt
1 (12-ounce) bag frozen peeled and deveined shrimp (28/31 count)
3 cups (24 ounces) baby spinach/arugula blend
1 tablespoon chopped fresh chives, for serving
Sriracha (optional), for serving

1. In a 7-inch round baking dish, whisk together the coconut milk, green curry paste, ginger, garlic, and pink salt. Add the shrimp and submerge in the coconut milk mixture. Cover tightly with foil.

2. Place a trivet with handles in the Instant Pot. Place the baking dish on the trivet.

3. Secure the lid on the pot and close the pressure-release valve. Set the pot to HIGH pressure for 7 minutes. At the end of the cooking time, quick-release the pressure. Select CANCEL.

4. Divide the greens between two shallow bowls. Top with the shrimp and curry sauce. Sprinkle with the chives. Serve with sriracha, if desired.

Per serving: Calories: 298 · Total Fat: 16 g · Protein: 26 g · Total Carbs: 8 g · Fiber: 2 g · Erythritol: 0 g · Net Carbs: 6 g

Chapter 8

Chicken

Clean Keto Chicken

This is another great dish for keto newbies as well as those looking to get back into ketosis—it's super filling, offers equal amounts of protein and fat, and has only 4 grams of net carbs. It's also incredibly easy to make and uses ingredients you probably have on hand. I like to use chicken thighs in this recipe because they have more fat and, in my opinion, more flavor than chicken breasts, but if you have chicken breasts in your fridge, go ahead and use them here. I like to pair this chicken with my Cajun Collard Greens and Pearl Onions (page 62) for a complete meal.

1. Place the lemon slices, wine, garlic, and ½ cup water in the Instant Pot. Season the chicken with ½ teaspoon of the thyme, the pink salt, and pepper. Place the chicken in the pot.

2. Secure the lid on the pot and close the pressure-release valve. Set the pot to **HIGH** pressure for 15 minutes. At the end of the cooking time, quick-release the pressure.

3. Open the pot and transfer the chicken thighs to a serving platter. Cover with foil to keep warm. Keep the lemon and garlic in the pot.

4. Select **SAUTÉ** and add the remaining ¼ teaspoon thyme, the butter, cream, and Parmesan. Simmer until the sauce is reduced and slightly thickened, 2 to 3 minutes. Select **CANCEL**.

5. To serve, pour the sauce over the chicken and sprinkle with additional Parmesan.

Per serving: Calories: 233 • Total Fat: 16 g • Protein: 16 g • Total Carbs: 5 g • Fiber: 1 g • Erythritol: 0 g • Net Carbs: 4 g

Serves: 4
Active prep time: 10 minutes
Cook time: 15 minutes

1 lemon, sliced
¼ cup white wine or chicken broth
2 cloves garlic, sliced
4 bone-in, skinless chicken thighs
¾ teaspoon dried thyme, divided
½ teaspoon fine Himalayan pink salt
½ teaspoon black pepper
2 tablespoons butter or ghee
¼ cup heavy cream
¼ cup grated Parmesan cheese (1 ounce), plus more for garnish

Chicken Enchilada Casserole

Before I went keto, I used to order chicken enchiladas every time I went to a Mexican restaurant. Now I can get those same comforting flavors from this super-easy casserole. To keep things simple, I use a jarred enchilada sauce (I usually buy Las Palmas or La Victoria). Be sure to read your labels carefully and avoid brands with added sugars.

Serves: 5
Active prep time: 15 minutes
Cook time: 22 minutes

3 boneless, skinless chicken breasts (or 3 cups precooked shredded chicken)
Fine Himalayan pink salt
1 (16-ounce) bag frozen cauliflower rice
3 tablespoons coconut flour
1 large egg, beaten
¼ teaspoon black pepper
1 (10-ounce) can red enchilada sauce
1 (4-ounce) can diced mild green chiles
2 teaspoons taco seasoning
1½ cups shredded cheddar or Mexican blend cheese
1 avocado, sliced, for serving
1 cup shredded lettuce, for serving
¼ cup sliced black olives, for serving

1. Pour 1 cup water into the Instant Pot. Place a trivet with handles in the pot. Season the chicken with pink salt and arrange on the trivet. Secure the lid on the pot and close the pressure-release valve. Set the pot to **HIGH** pressure for 10 minutes. At the end of the cooking time, quick-release the pressure. Transfer the breasts to a cutting board and shred with forks. Pour the water out of the Instant Pot.

2. In a microwave-safe dish, combine the cauliflower rice and ¼ cup water. Cover the dish with plastic wrap and steam in the microwave just until tender, about 3 minutes. Drain any excess water and transfer the cauliflower to a medium bowl. Stir in the coconut flour, egg, pepper, and ¼ teaspoon salt.

3. Coat a 7-inch round baking dish well with cooking spray. Pat the cauliflower mixture into the bottom of the dish.

4. In the medium bowl the cauliflower was mixed in, combine the shredded chicken, enchilada sauce, green chiles, and taco seasoning. Top the cauliflower base with the chicken mixture, then sprinkle with the cheese. Lightly coat a piece of foil with cooking spray and cover the dish with the foil.

5. Pour ¾ cup water into the Instant Pot. Place a trivet with handles in the pot and place the dish on the trivet. Secure the lid on the pot and close the pressure-release valve. Set the pot to **HIGH** pressure for 12 minutes. At the end of the cooking time, quick-release the pressure.

6. Carefully remove the trivet from the pot. Remove the foil and let stand for 10 minutes before serving, with avocado, lettuce, and olives as garnish.

Per serving: Calories: 430 • Total Fat: 25 g • Protein: 37 g • Total Carbs: 15 g • Fiber: 6 g • Erythritol: 0 g • Net Carbs: 9 g

Almond Pesto Chicken

I typically make pesto with almonds instead of pine nuts because I always have almonds stocked in my pantry—plus they're a lot more affordable than pine nuts. When pulsed in a food processor with fresh basil, olive oil, and Parmesan, you get a delicious pesto that's packed with healthy fats. This pesto pairs nicely with chicken and asparagus, but it's delicious with just about anything—try it as a sauce for veggie noodles or spoon a little over fish for an instant burst of flavor.

1. Select **SAUTÉ** on the Instant Pot. When the pot is hot, add 1 tablespoon of the olive oil. Add the mushrooms and cook for 1 minute. Add the asparagus and cook, stirring frequently, until the mushrooms are tender, about 4 minutes. Remove the vegetables from the pot and set aside.

2. Add 1 tablespoon of the olive oil to the pot. Sprinkle the chicken with pink salt and pepper. Cook the chicken until browned on both sides, about 3 minutes per side. Add the broth and use a spatula to scrape up any browned bits from the bottom of the pot. Select **CANCEL**.

3. Secure the lid on the pot and close the pressure-release valve. Set the pot to **HIGH** pressure for 8 minutes. At the end of the cooking time, use a natural release to depressurize.

4. Meanwhile, in a food processor, combine the basil, almonds, and garlic and pulse to coarsely chop. Add the remaining 3 tablespoons olive oil and process until almost smooth. Stir in the Parmesan. Season to taste with salt and pepper.

5. Remove the chicken from the pot along with all but 2 tablespoons of the cooking liquid. Select **SAUTÉ**. Add 1 teaspoon pesto and the mushroom-asparagus mixture to the reserved cooking liquid in the pot and toss. Spread the remaining pesto on top of the chicken and place on top of the vegetables in the pot. Cover with the lid and heat for 1 minute. Select **CANCEL**.

6. Serve the chicken over the asparagus and mushrooms with sauce spread over the top.

Serves: 4
Active prep time: 15 minutes
Cook time: 8 minutes

5 tablespoons olive oil
2 cups sliced button mushrooms
1 pound asparagus, trimmed and cut into 2-inch pieces
4 bone-in, skin-on chicken thighs (about 1½ pounds)
Fine Himalayan pink salt
Black pepper
¼ cup chicken broth
1 cup packed fresh basil leaves
2 tablespoons slivered almonds
1 clove garlic, peeled but whole
¼ cup grated Parmesan cheese

Per serving: Calories: 555 • Total Fat: 44 g • Protein: 35 g • Total Carbs: 7 g • Fiber: 3 g • Erythritol: 0 g • Net Carbs: 4 g

Creamy Bacon Ranch Chicken

In my early twenties, I loved to use dry ranch dressing mix on pretty much everything—it was budget friendly, low maintenance, and full of flavor. The truth is, I still love it! I've used it in this recipe to achieve that familiar ranch dressing flavor with minimal fuss. To change things up, you can swap in kale (you'll want to use about 4 cups) for the zucchini—the cook time remains the same, and stir in 1 teaspoon white wine vinegar after the cheddar has melted.

10 INGREDIENTS OR LESS

Serves: 4
Active prep time: 10 minutes
Cook time: 8 minutes

½ cup heavy cream
2 boneless, skinless chicken
   breasts (1¼ to 1½ pounds
   total)
2 tablespoons dry ranch
   dressing mix, divided
3 slices uncured bacon,
   chopped
1 cup chicken broth
8 ounces cream cheese, cubed
3 cups chopped zucchini
1½ cups shredded mild
   cheddar cheese

1. In a resealable plastic bag, combine the heavy cream, chicken, and 1½ tablespoons of the ranch dressing mix. Marinate in the refrigerator for 30 minutes.

2. Select **SAUTÉ** on the Instant Pot. Add the bacon and cook until crisp, 4 to 6 minutes. Transfer the bacon crumbles to paper towels to drain.

3. Remove the chicken from the marinade and place in the pot (discard the marinade). Cook the chicken for 2 minutes on each side or until lightly browned. Select **CANCEL**. Add the broth, cream cheese, and remaining ½ tablespoon ranch dressing mix to the pot.

4. Secure the lid on the pot and close the pressure-release valve. Set the pot to **HIGH** pressure for 8 minutes. At the end of the cooking time, quick-release the pressure. Transfer just the chicken breasts to a plate and cover to keep warm.

5. Whisk the sauce in the pot. Select **SAUTÉ**, add the zucchini, and simmer until the sauce is slightly reduced and the zucchini is tender, 5 to 7 minutes. Stir in the cheddar and heat until melted and the sauce is creamy. Select **CANCEL**.

6. Slice the chicken breast into strips and ladle the zucchini and sauce over chicken breasts. Top with the bacon crumbles.

Per serving: Calories: 730 • Total Fat: 54 g • Protein: 51 g • Total Carbs: 9 g • Fiber: 1 g • Erythritol: 0 g • Net Carbs: 8 g

Louisiana-Style Chicken Wings with Creamy Cucumber-Dill Dip

Wings are one of my main keto food groups (kidding, but not really), so I had to include a recipe in here for making them in the pressure cooker. For best results, marinate the drummies in all of those delicious flavors for as long as you can. I like to get them marinating before I leave for work in the morning so they're ready to throw in the Instant Pot when I get home.

1. In a large resealable plastic bag, combine the cream, vinegar, and Tabasco. Add the chicken and toss gently to coat. Marinate in the refrigerator for at least 2 hours or up to 24 hours.

2. In a small bowl, stir together the sour cream, cream cheese, cucumber, lemon juice, dill, pink salt, black pepper, and a dash of Tabasco. Cover and refrigerate until ready to serve.

3. When ready to cook, pour 1 cup water into the Instant Pot. Drain the chicken from the marinade and pat dry with paper towels. Place a trivet with handles in the pot. Arrange the wing pieces on the trivet.

4. Secure the lid on the pot and close the pressure-release valve. Set the pot to **HIGH** pressure for 10 minutes. At the end of the cooking time, quick-release the pressure.

5. Meanwhile, in a small bowl, stir together the garlic, bouillon powder, Italian seasoning, onion powder, and cayenne.

6. Position an oven rack 6 inches from the heat source and preheat the broiler to high. Line a large rimmed baking sheet with foil.

7. Open the Instant Pot and transfer the wing pieces to the baking sheet. In a microwave-safe bowl, heat the butter for 40 seconds or until melted. Brush the wing pieces with ¼ cup of the melted butter and sprinkle with half of the seasoning mixture. Broil until browned, about 4 minutes. Turn the pieces over and brush with the remaining butter and sprinkle with the remaining seasoning mixture. Broil until the second side is browned, 3 to 4 minutes more.

8. Serve with the dip.

Serves: 4
Active prep time: 20 minutes
Cook time: 10 minutes

2 cups heavy cream
¼ cup apple cider vinegar
2 tablespoons Tabasco or other similar hot sauce, plus a dash for the dip
2 pounds chicken drumettes, flats, or a mix
½ cup sour cream
4 tablespoons cream cheese, at room temperature
¼ cup grated cucumber
1 tablespoon fresh lemon juice
2 teaspoons dried dill weed
1⅛ teaspoon fine Himalayan pink salt
⅛ teaspoon black pepper
1½ teaspoons granulated garlic
1½ teaspoons keto-friendly chicken bouillon powder
1½ teaspoons Italian seasoning
½ teaspoon onion powder
½ teaspoon cayenne pepper
8 tablespoons butter

Per serving: Calories: 685 • Total Fat: 62 g • Protein: 27 g • Total Carbs: 7 g • Fiber: 0 g • Erythritol: 0 g • Net Carbs: 7 g

Chicken Parmesan Meatballs

It's hard to go wrong with meatballs, but this particular version makes me happy on so many levels. The meatballs are tender and juicy, and once covered in a nice cozy blanket of tomato sauce and melted mozzarella, they're pretty hard to resist. I like to serve them over sautéed zucchini noodles or in radicchio or cabbage leaves to add a little texture and crunch.

Serves: 4
Active prep time: 15 minutes
Cook time: 10 minutes

1 large egg
2 cups shredded mozzarella
   cheese (8 ounces)
½ cup grated Parmesan
   cheese (2 ounces)
½ cup crushed pork rinds or
   almond meal
2 tablespoons chopped fresh
   basil, plus ¼ cup thinly sliced
   fresh basil for garnish
2 cloves garlic, minced
1½ pounds ground chicken
4 tablespoons olive oil, divided
1 tablespoon tomato paste
1 (14.5-ounce) can whole
   peeled plum (Italian)
   tomatoes, undrained
1 teaspoon dried basil, crushed
1 teaspoon garlic powder

1. In a medium bowl, combine the egg, 1 cup of the mozzarella, the Parmesan, pork rinds, chopped basil, and garlic. Add the chicken and mix gently using your hands to combine. Form into 28 meatballs about 1½ inches in diameter.

2. Select **SAUTÉ** on the Instant Pot. When the pot is hot, add 2 tablespoons of the olive oil. Add about half of the meatballs to the hot oil and cook until browned on all sides, turning the meatballs as needed, 6 to 8 minutes. Transfer the meatballs to a plate. Repeat with the remaining meatballs and 2 tablespoons olive oil.

3. Add the tomato paste to the pot. Cook and stir for 1 minute. Add the canned tomatoes and their juice, breaking them apart as you do so. Stir in the dried basil and garlic powder. Return the meatballs to the pot. Select **CANCEL**.

4. Secure the lid on the pot and close the pressure-release valve. Set the pot to **HIGH** pressure for 10 minutes. At the end of the cooking time, use a natural release to depressurize.

5. Top the meatballs with the remaining 1 cup mozzarella and let stand until melted before serving with the basil leaves.

Per serving: Calories: 651 • Total Fat: 42 g • Protein: 60 g • Total Carbs: 10 g • Fiber: 2 g • Erythritol: 0 g • Net Carbs: 8 g

Indian Butter Chicken

I've avoided Indian restaurants since I've been keto, mostly because I don't trust myself around naan bread. Luckily, this recipe for butter chicken gives me all the same tastes far away from the bread basket. I like to pair it with sautéed cauliflower rice and additional cilantro to complete the experience.

1. Season the chicken with 1 teaspoon of the pink salt and pepper. Select **SAUTÉ** on the Instant Pot. Add 1 tablespoon of the butter, and the minced garlic. When the butter is melted and hot, add half of the chicken in a single layer. Cook until browned on both sides, 6 to 8 minutes, turning once. Remove the chicken from the pot and repeat with the remaining chicken and 1 additional tablespoon of butter.

2. Add the onion and jalapeño to the pot. Cook, stirring often, until tender, 2 to 3 minutes. Stir in the garam masala, ginger, cumin, turmeric, and ¾ teaspoon pink salt. Cook for 1 minute. Return the chicken to the pot. Select **CANCEL**.

3. Secure the lid on the pot and close the pressure-release valve. Set the pot to **HIGH** pressure for 10 minutes. At the end of the cooking time, use a natural release for 10 minutes to depressurize, then quick-release the remaining pressure.

4. Stir in the cream, cilantro, and the remaining butter.

Per serving: Calories: 613 · Total Fat: 44 g · Protein: 47 g · Total Carbs: 6 g · Fiber: 1 g · Erythritol: 0 g · Net Carbs: 5 g

Serves: 4
Active prep time: 10 minutes
Cook time: 10 minutes

2 pounds boneless, skinless chicken thighs
1 teaspoon plus ¾ teaspoon fine Himalayan pink salt, divided
½ teaspoon cracked black pepper
4 tablespoons butter or ghee, divided
2 cloves garlic, minced
1 small onion, chopped
1 jalapeño pepper, finely chopped (seeded if desired)
1 tablespoon garam masala
2 teaspoons minced fresh ginger
1 teaspoon ground cumin
1 teaspoon ground turmeric
1 cup heavy cream or coconut cream
¼ cup chopped fresh cilantro

Shredded Green Chile Chicken Bowl

This bowl has all of the good stuff in it—it's a little spicy, a lot savory, and just so, so delicious. I usually use shredded chicken thighs for this dish, but I've also tried it with cubed pork shoulder (the cook time remains the same) and it's pretty amazing. If you like to live on the spicy side, I recommend topping off your bowl with some sliced jalapeños.

Serves: 4
Active prep time: 20 minutes
Cook time: 9 minutes

1½ pounds boneless, skinless chicken thighs
1 tablespoon taco seasoning
½ teaspoon fine Himalayan pink salt, divided
½ teaspoon black pepper
2 tablespoons avocado oil
½ cup salsa verde
1 (4-ounce) can mild diced green chiles, undrained
3 cups cauliflower rice
¾ cup chicken broth
Grated zest of 1 lime
Juice of 2 limes, divided
¼ cup chopped fresh cilantro
1 avocado, diced
2 green onions, chopped
1 cup shredded cheddar or pepper Jack cheese
½ cup sour cream
Jalapeños, sliced (optional)

1. Season the chicken on both sides with the taco seasoning, half of the pink salt, and pepper. Select **SAUTÉ** on the Instant Pot. When the pot is hot, add the avocado oil. Add the chicken thighs to the hot oil and brown on both sides, 5 to 6 minutes total. Press **CANCEL**. Pour the salsa verde and chiles over the chicken.

2. Secure the lid on the pot and close the pressure-release valve. Set the pot to **HIGH** pressure for 8 minutes. Select a natural release to depressurize.

3. Transfer the chicken to a bowl or cutting board and use two forks to shred into bite-size pieces. Transfer the cooking liquid from the Instant Pot to a bowl and stir in the chicken. Cover to keep warm.

4. Add the cauliflower rice, broth, lime zest, and half of the lime juice to the pot. Secure the lid on the pot and close the pressure-release valve. Set the pot to **HIGH** pressure for 1 minute. At the end of the cooking time, quick-release the pressure. Open the pot and stir in the cilantro. Cover and keep warm.

5. In a bowl, combine the avocado, green onions, remaining lime juice, and remaining pink salt.

6. To serve, divide the cauliflower rice among four bowls. Top with the chicken, cooking liquid, avocado mixture, cheese, sour cream, and jalapeños, if desired.

Per serving: Calories: 526 • Total Fat: 33 g • Protein: 44 g • Total Carbs: 14 g • Fiber: 5 g • Erythritol: 0 g • Net Carbs: 9 g

Chicken with Pancetta and Broccoli

Pancetta is the secret ingredient in a lot of my favorite keto recipes—just a little bit goes a long way, and its salty flavor adds depth and extra crave-ability to so many dishes. Here I use it as a crispy topping for simply prepared chicken and broccoli covered in a creamy cheese sauce. This is definitely one of the richer dinners in this book, and it is a good one to try if you are following an OMAD (one meal a day) plan or are incorporating intermittent fasting into your routine.

1. Select **SAUTÉ** on the Instant Pot. When the pot is hot, add the olive oil. Add the pancetta to the hot oil and cook until the pieces are crisp, 3 to 4 minutes. Transfer to paper towels to drain. Select **CANCEL**.

2. Remove all but about 2 tablespoons of the oil from the pot. Select **SAUTÉ**. Add the onion and garlic. Cook, stirring occasionally, until tender, 2 to 3 minutes. Select **CANCEL**.

3. Add the broth to the pot. Season the chicken breasts with the Italian seasoning, pepper flakes, pink salt, and black pepper. Add the chicken to the pot.

4. Secure the lid on the pot and close the pressure-release valve. Set the pot to **HIGH** pressure for 15 minutes. At the end of the cooking time, quick-release the pressure. Transfer the chicken to a plate and cover to keep warm.

5. Select **SAUTÉ** and add the broccoli and cream. Simmer until the sauce is slightly thickened, about 4 minutes. Add the Gouda and Swiss cheeses and stir until melted. Select **CANCEL**.

6. Slice the chicken breasts before serving. Spoon the sauce over the chicken and sprinkle with the pancetta.

Per serving: Calories: 745 • Total Fat: 44 g • Protein: 72 g • Total Carbs: 14 g • Fiber: 4 g • Erythritol: 0 g • Net Carbs: 10 g

Serves: 3
Active prep time: 10 minutes
Cook time: 15 minutes

1 tablespoon olive oil
2 ounces pancetta, diced
½ cup diced onion
1 tablespoon minced garlic
¾ cup chicken broth
2 boneless, skinless chicken breasts (about 1 ¼ pounds total)
2 teaspoons Italian seasoning
¼ teaspoon crushed red pepper flakes
¼ teaspoon fine Himalayan pink salt
¼ teaspoon black pepper
2 cups small broccoli florets
¼ cup heavy cream
½ cup shredded Gouda cheese (2 ounces)
¼ cup shredded Swiss cheese (1 ounce)

Lemon-Pepper Chicken

This simple, anytime meal has only 1 net carb, and takes just 20 minutes to cook. I love making a whole chicken as opposed to just the breast or thighs, as it provides so much meat and I can use the leftover cooking liquid to make homemade gravy. Here's how: After removing the chicken and the trivet from the pot, select **SAUTÉ** and bring your cooking liquid to a boil. In a small bowl whisk together 2 tablespoons arrowroot or cornstarch and ⅓ cup cool water. Whisk into the cooking liquid and cook until thickened. Voila! You can pour your gravy into silicone molds and freeze it into cubes.

10 INGREDIENTS OR LESS

Serves: 4
Active prep time: 15 minutes
Cook time: 20 minutes

1 whole chicken (3 pounds)
2 large cloves garlic, thinly
  sliced
1 lemon
3 tablespoons butter or ghee,
  melted, divided
2 teaspoons dried thyme
1 teaspoon fine Himalayan pink
  salt
¼ teaspoon black pepper
1 cup chicken broth

1. With a paring knife, make small cuts all over the chicken thigh and drumstick skin. Insert a slice of garlic into each cut, and also place under the skin of the breast. Grate 2 teaspoons zest from the lemon and set aside. Cut the lemon in half and rub the chicken with the lemon halves, then place the halves in the cavity. Brush the chicken with 2 tablespoons of the melted butter. Tie the legs together with cotton kitchen string. In a small bowl, combine the lemon zest, thyme, pink salt, and pepper and rub all over the chicken.

2. Pour the broth into the Instant Pot. Place a trivet with handles in the pot. Place the chicken breast-side up on the trivet.

3. Secure the lid on the pot and close the pressure-release valve. Set the pot to **HIGH** pressure for 20 minutes. At the end of the cooking time, use a natural release to depressurize. An instant-read thermometer should read at least 165°F when inserted in the thigh.

4. Position an oven rack so the breast of the chicken will be 6 inches from the heat source and preheat the broiler. Transfer the chicken to a large baking pan and brush with the remaining 1 tablespoon melted butter. Untie the legs and discard the lemon halves. Broil the chicken until browned, 4 to 5 minutes.

5. Serve the chicken with the cooking liquid, if desired.

Pressure Cooker Tip: A handy guideline for cooking a whole chicken is roughly 6 minutes per pound at high pressure.

Per serving: Calories: 569 • Total Fat: 43 g • Protein: 43 g • Total Carbs: 1 g • Fiber: 0 g • Erythritol: 0 g • Net Carbs: 1 g

Pork

Tequila-Lime Carnitas

This tequila-infused carnitas recipe is perfect for festive occasions—or any weeknight you want to party. It's also a great way to feed a crowd and is super simple to scale up—I make double or triple batches any time I have people over because everyone always wants seconds and thirds! I like to set out a spread of toppings, including queso fresco, chopped avocado, and sour cream, but you can choose any toppings you prefer. Also, if you are avoiding alcohol, feel free to swap out the tequila for additional broth.

1. Rub the pork pieces evenly with the chile-lime seasoning. Place the pork in the Instant Pot. Add the broth, tequila, and 2 tablespoons of the lime juice.

2. Secure the lid on the pot and close the pressure-release valve. Set the pot to **HIGH** pressure for 60 minutes. At the end of the cooking time, use a natural release to depressurize.

3. Using a slotted spoon, transfer the pork from the pot to a bowl. Use two forks to shred it into large bite-size pieces. Pour the cooking juices out of the pot into a separate bowl.

4. Wipe out the pot. Select **SAUTÉ** and when the pot is hot, add 1 tablespoon of the avocado oil. Add about half of the pork to the hot oil and cook, stirring occasionally, until the pork is browned and slightly crisp in some places, about 15 minutes. Remove the pork from the pot. Repeat with the remaining pork and 1 tablespoon avocado oil. Return all the pork to the pot and season to taste with salt. Select **CANCEL**.

5. Stir the cilantro, lime zest, and remaining 2 tablespoons lime juice into the pork. Skim the fat from the reserved cooking juices and add the cooking juices as desired to moisten the carnitas.

6. Serve the carnitas with butter lettuce leaves and desired toppings.

Per serving: Calories: 447 • Total Fat: 17 g • Protein: 59 g • Total Carbs: 4 g • Fiber: 1 g • Erythritol: 0 • Net Carbs: 3 g

10 INGREDIENTS OR LESS

Serves: 4
Active prep time: 15 minutes
Cook time: 60 minutes

2½- to 3-pound boneless pork butt roast, cut into 3 or 4 large pieces
2 tablespoons chile-lime seasoning (like Tajín)
½ cup chicken or beef broth
¼ cup 100% agave tequila
4 tablespoons fresh lime juice, divided
2 tablespoons avocado oil
Fine Himalayan pink salt
½ cup chopped fresh cilantro
1 teaspoon grated lime zest
2 small heads butter lettuce
Toppings, such as queso fresco, avocado, sour cream, and/or hot sauce (Note: Nutritional information does not include toppings.)

Parmesan and Pork Rind Crusted Pork Chops

I often make pork chops for my family—they're affordable, cook quickly, and are delicious when given a little love. Crushed pork rinds are an excellent replacement for bread crumbs, and they make a killer crust. These chops are super satisfying and are high in calories, so they're a good option. I like to serve them with a simple salad of arugula or mixed greens drizzled with olive oil and lemon juice.

Serves: 2
Active prep time: 15 minutes
Cook time: 5 minutes

2 boneless pork loin chops, about 1 inch thick
¼ teaspoon fine Himalayan pink salt
¼ teaspoon black pepper
⅔ cup finely crushed pork rinds
1½ teaspoons Italian seasoning
1 large egg
3 tablespoons almond flour
1 tablespoon olive oil
2 tablespoons grated Parmesan cheese
1 teaspoon lemon zest
1 teaspoon dried parsley

1. Season the pork chops on both sides with pink salt and pepper. Pour 1 cup water into the Instant Pot. Place a trivet with handles in the pot. Set the chops on the trivet.

2. Secure the lid on the pot and close the pressure-release valve. Select **MANUAL** and set the pot to **HIGH** pressure for 5 minutes. At the end of the cooking time, quick release the pressure. Remove the chops and trivet from the pot. Discard any remaining water and wipe out the pot.

3. In a shallow dish or pie plate, combine the crushed pork rinds and Italian seasoning. In a second shallow dish, whisk together the egg and 1 tablespoon water. Place the almond flour in a third shallow dish. Coat both sides of each chop in the almond flour, then the egg mixture, and finally the pork rind mixture.

4. Select **SAUTÉ** on the Instant Pot. When the pot is hot, add the oil. When the oil is hot, add the chops and cook on both sides until browned, about 5 minutes. Select **CANCEL**.

5. Meanwhile, in a small bowl combine the Parmesan, lemon zest, and parsley.

6. Sprinkle the hot chops with the Parmesan mixture to serve.

Per serving: Calories: 653 • Total Fat: 37 g • Protein: 74 g • Total Carbs: 4 g • Fiber: 2 g • Erythritol: 0 g • Net Carbs: 2 g

Pork Belly Ramen with Veggie Noodles

Just because I can't eat traditional noodles doesn't mean I can't re-create a keto-friendly version of my favorite steamy bowl of ramen with veggie noodles. For me, the best part about ramen is the Pho-inspired toppings, especially the soft-cooked egg added just before serving. Fresh herbs, jalapeño, and lime juice are a few of my other favorites, but you do you!

1. In a small bowl, combine the pork belly and coconut aminos. Turn the pork over to coat both sides. If desired, sprinkle with erythritol to add a bit of sweetness. Let stand 10 minutes.

2. Select **SAUTÉ** on the Instant Pot. When the pot is hot, add the avocado oil. Add the onion and garlic to the hot oil and cook, stirring occasionally, for 3 minutes. Select **CANCEL**. Scrape the onion mixture into a bowl.

3. Select **SAUTÉ**. Add the pork belly to the pot, reserving the marinade. Cook until golden, carefully turning to brown all sides, about 3 minutes. Immediately add the broth, stirring to release any browned bits on the bottom of the pot. Return the onion mixture to the pot and add the mushrooms, reserved marinade, and ginger. Select **CANCEL**.

4. Secure the lid on the pot and close the pressure-release valve. Set the pot to **HIGH** pressure for 30 minutes. At the end of the cooking time, quick-release the pressure. Transfer the pork belly to a cutting board and slice. You can slice into four larger pieces or eight smaller chunks. Cover to keep warm.

5. Select **SAUTÉ** on the Instant Pot. Return the cooking liquid and mushrooms to a boil. Add the zucchini noodles and cook just until the zucchini noodles are crisp-tender, about 3 minutes.

6. Divide the pork belly into soup bowls. Ladle the soup over the pork belly. Top with a soft-boiled egg half, green onions, and desired toppings.

Per serving: Calories: 639 • Total Fat: 59 g • Protein: 16 g • Total Carbs: 11 g • Fiber: 2 g • Erythritol: 0 g • Net Carbs: 9 g

Serves: 4
Active prep time: 15 minutes
Cook time: 36 minutes

1 pound center-cut pork belly
1 tablespoon coconut aminos, tamari, or soy sauce
¼ teaspoon erythritol (optional)
1 teaspoon avocado oil
½ cup coarsely chopped onion
3 cloves garlic, peeled and halved
6 cups beef or chicken broth
2 cups shiitake mushrooms, stems removed, caps sliced
2 tablespoons grated fresh ginger
1 (10- to 12-ounce) package zucchini or summer squash noodles
2 large eggs, soft-boiled, peeled and halved
¼ cup sliced green onion, for serving
Toppings, such as chopped fresh mint and/or cilantro, seeded and chopped jalapeño, and lime wedges (optional)

Sour Cream Dijon Pork Chops

Dijon and pork are a match made in heaven, and this rich sour cream/Dijon sauce truly transforms everyday pork chops into something special. I like to add a side of cauliflower rice or some sautéed zucchini noodles to get in more veggies—and to sop up the extra sauce! Note that real Dijon mustard doesn't contain a lot of added sugars (and is not the same thing as honey mustard)—look for a brand like Grey Poupon, which has 0 grams of carbs.

10 INGREDIENTS OR LESS

Serves: 4
Active prep time: 10 minutes
Cook time: 5 minutes

2 boneless pork chops, 1 to
   1¼ inches thick
¼ teaspoon each fine
   Himalayan pink salt and
   black pepper
1 tablespoon olive oil
1 cup chopped yellow onion
2 cloves garlic, minced
1 cup chicken broth
1 cup sour cream
1 (5-ounce) package baby
   spinach
2 tablespoons Dijon mustard
4 teaspoons grated Parmesan
   cheese

1. Season both sides of the pork chops evenly with the pink salt and pepper.

2. Select **SAUTÉ** on the Instant Pot. When the pot is hot, add the olive oil. Add the pork chops to the hot oil and cook until browned on both sides, 4 to 5 minutes (see Tip). Select **CANCEL**. Do not remove the chops. Add the onion, garlic, and broth to the pot.

3. Secure the lid on the pot and close the pressure-release valve. Set the pot to **HIGH** pressure for 5 minutes. At the end of the cooking time, quick-release the pressure. Open the pot and transfer the pork chops to a serving platter. Cover with foil to keep warm.

4. Select **SAUTÉ**. Stir in the sour cream, spinach, and mustard. Heat for 2 to 3 minutes to wilt the spinach and warm the sauce through.

5. Spoon the sauce and spinach over the chops and sprinkle with the Parmesan.

Pressure Cooker Tip: Sauté the chops in batches if they are too large for the 6-quart Instant Pot. Add 2 teaspoons additional olive oil when sautéing the second batch.

Per serving: Calories: 310 • Total Fat: 17 g • Protein: 29 g • Total Carbs: 9 g • Fiber: 1 g • Erythritol: 0 g • Net Carbs: 8 g

Pork Chops and Quick 'Kraut

This dish is a play on the classic combination of pork and sauerkraut, with a quick 'kraut made from red cabbage, vinegar, mustard, and thyme that takes minutes to pull together. For some extra kick, I like to add a teaspoon of sweet paprika to my 'kraut. Make this easy but delicious dish for good luck on New Year's Day—or any day of the week!

1. Select **SAUTÉ** on the Instant Pot. When the pot is hot, add the butter and garlic. Sprinkle the pork chops with pink salt and pepper. Add the chops to the hot garlic butter and brown until golden, about 2 minutes per side (see Tip on page 150). Select **CANCEL**. Remove the chops.

2. Make the sauerkraut: Add the cabbage, vinegar, ¼ cup water, ½ tablespoon of the mustard, and ½ tablespoon of the thyme to the drippings in the pot. Whisk to release any browned bits on the bottom of the pot. Top with the chops and spread them with the remaining ½ tablespoon mustard and sprinkle with the remaining ½ tablespoon thyme.

3. Secure the lid on the pot and close the pressure-relief valve. Set the pot to **HIGH** pressure for 9 minutes. At the end of the cooking time, use a natural release to depressurize for 10 minutes, then quick-release the remaining pressure. An instant-read thermometer inserted in the pork chops should read 145°F. If the pork chops are less than 145°F, secure the lid and let stand with the pot off for 2 to 4 minutes.

4. Serve the pork chops over the sauerkraut.

Per serving: Calories: 315 • Total Fat: 11 g • Protein: 37 g • Total Carbs: 12 g • Fiber: 3 g • Erythritol: 0 g • Net Carbs: 9 g

10 INGREDIENTS OR LESS

Serves: 2
Active prep time: 10 minutes
Cook time: 9 minutes

1 to 2 tablespoons butter or ghee
1 clove garlic, minced
2 bone-in center-cut pork chops, 1 inch thick
Fine Himalayan pink salt and black pepper

For the sauerkraut:

1 (10-ounce) package shredded red or green cabbage (about 3 cups)
3 tablespoons apple cider vinegar
1 tablespoon whole-grain mustard or Dijon mustard, divided
1 tablespoon fresh thyme or 1 teaspoon dried thyme, crushed, divided

Kālua Pork

Does dinner get any easier than a recipe with just three ingredients? This dish was inspired by my time in Hawaii—my family lived on Oahu for nine years, and I absolutely fell in love with the local flavors and culture while I was there. This is a straight-up protein feast with 0 net carbs—I like to pair the smoky pork with lettuce wraps, red cabbage, or a quick sauté of baby spinach. No matter how you serve it, be sure to drizzle the shredded pork with the *kālua* cooking liquid—it's full of flavor!

10 INGREDIENTS OR LESS

Serves: 6
Active prep time: 5 minutes
Cook time: 1 hour 5 minutes

4 pounds boneless pork butt roast
4 teaspoons fine Himalayan pink salt
2 tablespoons liquid smoke

1. Rub the entire pork roast with the pink salt. Let sit 5 minutes. Pour 1 cup water into the Instant Pot. Place the pork roast into the pot and sprinkle with the liquid smoke.

2. Secure the lid on the pot and close the pressure-release valve. Set the pot to HIGH pressure for 65 minutes. At the end of the cooking time, use a natural release to depressurize.

3. Transfer the pork to a cutting board or serving platter. Use two forks to shred the pork. Ladle a small amount of the cooking liquid over the pork right before serving.

Per serving: Calories: 360 • Total Fat: 11 g • Protein: 61 g • Total Carbs: 0 g • Fiber: 0 g • Erythritol: 0 g • Net Carbs: 0 g

Pesto Pizza Casserole

This dish offers all of the flavors of a meat lover's pizza, minus the carbs. Feel free to swap in any of your favorite meats here—you could do prosciutto instead of cubed ham, or ground beef in place of sausage. But pepperoni is a nonnegotiable—it's what makes this casserole truly reminiscent of pizza! You can also customize with your favorite pizza toppings, such as sliced olives, mushrooms, red pepper flakes, or fresh basil—kids especially love this DIY part of the "pizza" experience!

1. Place the shredded zucchini in a colander, sprinkle with the pink salt, and toss to coat. Place the colander in another bowl and let stand 15 minutes. Press and squeeze excess liquid from the zucchini and pat dry with paper towels.

2. Meanwhile, select **SAUTÉ** on the Instant Pot. Add the bacon and ham and cook, stirring occasionally, until lightly browned, about 5 minutes. Use a slotted spoon to transfer the bacon and ham to a medium bowl. Add the Italian sausage to the pot and cook, stirring occasionally, until cooked through, about 5 minutes. Select **CANCEL**. Use a slotted spoon to transfer the sausage to the bowl with the ham and bacon. Stir in the pepperoni.

3. Grease a 7-inch round baking dish with the butter. If you want to transfer the dish for serving, use a springform pan. In a medium bowl, combine the drained and squeezed zucchini, the egg, Parmesan, almond meal, and Italian seasoning. Transfer to the prepared baking dish and press into the bottom to form a crust. Spoon the pesto over the zucchini "crust." Top with the meat mixture and provolone. Cover the baking dish tightly with foil.

4. Pour 1 cup water into the pot. Place a trivet with handles in the pot and place the baking dish on the trivet. Secure the lid on the pot and close the pressure-release valve. Set the pot to **HIGH** pressure for 15 minutes. At the end of the cooking time, use a natural release to depressurize.

5. Allow the casserole to stand for 15 minutes before serving.

Serves: 4
Active prep time: 20 minutes
Cook time: 15 minutes

1 medium zucchini, coarsely shredded
¾ teaspoon fine Himalayan pink salt
4 slices uncured bacon, chopped
8 ounces cubed ham
8 ounces Italian sausage
¼ cup mini pepperoni slices
1 tablespoon butter or ghee
1 large egg
½ cup grated Parmesan cheese (2 ounces)
⅓ cup almond flour or almond meal
1 teaspoon Italian seasoning
⅓ cup prepared basil pesto
1½ cups shredded provolone cheese (6 ounces)

Per serving: Calories: 726 · Total Fat: 59 g · Protein: 39 g · Total Carbs: 10 g · Fiber: 2 g · Erythritol: 0 g · Net Carbs: 8 g

Chorizo Meatloaf

Spicy chorizo—a sausage flavored with garlic, paprika, and salt—adds a nice punch of flavor to this Mexican take on meatloaf. Most traditional recipes call for beef, but I like using lean ground pork mixed with the fattier sausage *and* mushrooms (which have a high water content) to create a really succulent meatloaf with great texture. A little bit of cheese and fresh avocado finish things off for a south-of-the-border take on this old-time classic like you've never had before!

10 INGREDIENTS OR LESS

Serves: 4
Active prep time: 10 minutes
Cook time: 25 minutes

1 pound lean ground pork
6 ounces Mexican chorizo,
   casings removed, crumbled
¾ cup finely chopped
   mushrooms
1½ cups shredded pepper Jack
   cheese (6 ounces), divided
2 large eggs
¼ cup salsa, plus more for
   serving
2 tablespoons chopped
   fresh cilantro, plus more for
   serving
2 teaspoons taco seasoning
Sliced or mashed avocado,
   for serving (optional) (Note:
   Nutritional information does
   not include the avocado.)

1. Coat a 7-inch round baking dish or loaf pan with cooking spray. In a large bowl, combine the pork, chorizo, mushrooms, 1 cup of the pepper Jack, the eggs, salsa, cilantro, and taco seasoning. Mix gently to combine. Transfer to the prepared dish and lightly press with the back of a spoon. Cover the dish with foil.

2. Pour ½ cup water into the Instant Pot. Place a trivet with handles in the pot. Place the foil-wrapped meatloaf on the trivet.

3. Secure the lid on the pot and close the pressure-release valve. Set the pot to **HIGH** pressure for 25 minutes. At the end of the cooking time, use a natural release to depressurize for 15 minutes, then quick-release the remaining pressure. An instant-read thermometer inserted in the meatloaf should read 160°F. (If not up to temperature, secure the lid and let stand for 5 minutes.) Remove the meatloaf from the dish (discard the cooking liquid).

4. Slice the meatloaf and sprinkle the servings with the remaining ½ cup pepper Jack. Serve with salsa, cilantro, and avocado, if desired.

Per serving: Calories: 653 • Total Fat: 49 g • Protein: 43 g • Total Carbs: 4 g • Fiber: 1 g • Erythritol: 0 g • Net Carbs: 3 g

Ginger-Lime Baby Back Ribs

Ribs are the easiest way to my daughter's heart. She orders them whenever we go out to eat, so I've started making them at home, too. I like to serve these mouthwatering ribs alongside a simple slaw made with shredded cabbage, lime juice, and avocado oil mayonnaise. This is a really solid yet simple meal that will keep your macros in line and make you feel like you're not giving up a thing.

1. Place a trivet with handles in the Instant Pot. Add the broth and 1 tablespoon of the lime juice. Pat the ribs dry with paper towels. Remove the thin membrane from the back of the ribs. Cut the ribs into 4 sections. In a small bowl, combine chili powder, ginger, garlic, pink salt, and pepper. Rub the spice mixture evenly over the ribs. Arrange the ribs on the trivet.

2. Secure the lid on the pot and close the pressure-release valve. Set the pot to **HIGH** pressure for 25 minutes. At the end of the cooking time, use a natural release to depressurize.

3. Meanwhile, make the sauce: In a small saucepan, combine the coconut aminos, butter, sesame oil, lime zest, and remaining 2 tablespoons lime juice. Cook the sauce over medium-low heat just until the butter melts, about 2 minutes.

4. Adjust an oven rack to 6 inches from the heat source. Preheat the broiler. Line a large baking sheet with foil.

5. Open the Instant Pot and transfer the ribs, meaty-side down, to the prepared baking sheet (discard the cooking liquid from the pot). Brush the ribs with some of the sauce. Broil until browned, 3 to 4 minutes. Turn the ribs over. Brush with more sauce. Broil until browned and slightly charred, 3 to 4 minutes more.

6. In a small bowl, toss together all ingredients for the slaw.

7. To serve, brush the ribs with any remaining sauce and sprinkle with the green onion and sesame seeds. Serve with slaw.

Per serving: Calories: 354 • Total Fat: 26 g • Protein: 25 g • Total Carbs: 6 g • Fiber: 1 g • Erythritol: 0 g • Net Carbs: 5 g

Serves: 4
Active prep time: 15 minutes
Cook time: 25 minutes

¾ cup chicken broth
3 tablespoons fresh lime juice, divided
2 to 2½-pound rack baby back ribs
2 tablespoons chili powder
2 tablespoons minced fresh ginger
3 cloves garlic, minced
1½ teaspoons fine Himalayan pink salt
1 teaspoon black pepper

For the sauce:
¼ cup coconut aminos, tamari, or soy sauce
4 tablespoons butter
2 teaspoons toasted sesame oil
1 teaspoon grated lime zest
¼ cup sliced green onion
2 teaspoons sesame seeds
Simple Slaw (optional; recipe follows)

For the slaw:
½ pound green or red cabbage, shredded
Juice of ½ lime
1 to 2 tablespoons avocado oil mayonnaise
Pinch of fine Himalayan pink salt

Bacon Cauliflower "Mac" and Cheese

Cheesy cauliflower and crispy bacon? Sign me up! This keto-friendly take on mac and cheese is like a big, warm hug in a bowl. I love a crispy top on mine, so I like to finish this dish off under the broiler for 2 minutes in an ovenproof 1½-quart baking dish after sprinkling with crushed pork rinds. The added salty flavor and crunchy texture take this dish to another level.

10 INGREDIENTS OR LESS

Serves: 4
Active prep time: 10 minutes
Cook time: 1 minute

4 cups cauliflower florets
4 slices uncured bacon, diced
¾ cup heavy cream
2 ounces cream cheese
2 teaspoons dry ranch
 dressing mix
2 teaspoons Dijon mustard
Pinch of cayenne pepper
¼ teaspoon fine Himalayan
 pink salt
1½ cups shredded cheddar
 cheese

1. Pour 1 cup water into the Instant Pot. Put a vegetable steamer basket in the pot. Arrange the cauliflower in the basket.

2. Secure the lid on the pot and close the pressure-release valve. Set the pot to HIGH pressure for 1 minute. At the end of the cooking time, quick-release the pressure. Remove the cauliflower and steamer basket from the pot and set aside.

3. Pour off any water in the pot. Select SAUTÉ. Add the bacon and cook, stirring frequently, until crisp, 4 to 6 minutes. Add the cream, cream cheese, ranch dressing mix, mustard, cayenne, and pink salt. Cook until the cream cheese melts, then gradually add the cheddar, stirring constantly until smooth. Select CANCEL.

4. Add the cooked cauliflower and toss gently to coat with the cheese mixture. Divide among four bowls and top with additional bacon crumbles if you wish.

Per serving: Calories: 562 · Total Fat: 51 g · Protein: 19 g · Total Carbs: 9 g · Fiber: 2 g · Erythritol: 0 g · Net Carbs: 7 g

Beef

Mexican Meatballs

Meatballs are universally delicious. You can infuse them with flavors from various regions and cultures, and they always bring people together. These meatballs are inspired by Mexican flavors: garlic, cumin, chipotle powder, and a little taco seasoning for good measure to create a spicy meatball that then gets topped any way you like. In addition to my go-to Mexican toppings of cheese, sour cream, and avocado, I like to add a few pickled red onion slices.

1. In a large bowl, combine the ground beef, crushed pork rinds, egg, chipotle powder, garlic powder, onion powder, and cumin. Mix well. Form into twelve 1½-inch meatballs. Set aside.

2. In a small bowl, stir together the tomato sauce, taco seasoning, and pink salt. Set aside.

3. Select SAUTÉ on the Instant Pot. When the pot is hot, add the avocado oil. Working in two batches if necessary (take care not to overcrowd the pot), add the meatballs to the hot oil and brown on all sides, 3 to 5 minutes. Remove to a plate and cover with foil.

4. Pour off all but about 2 tablespoons of the fat from the pot. When the pot is hot again, add the seasoned tomato sauce, taking care to avoid the hot splatter. Simmer for 3 minutes. Select CANCEL. Return the meatballs to the pot.

5. Secure the lid on the pot and close the pressure-release valve. Set the pot to HIGH pressure for 7 minutes. At the end of the cooking time, use a natural release for 10 minutes to depressurize, then quick-release the remaining pressure.

6. While the meatballs cook, make the Quick Pickled Onions. In a small jar, combine all ingredients. Let sit 15 minutes.

7. Serve 3 meatballs on one or two butter lettuce leaves with desired toppings and the pickled onions.

Per serving: Calories: 396 • Total Fat: 30 g • Protein: 27 g • Total Carbs: 5 g • Fiber: 1 g • Erythritol: 0 g • Net Carbs: 4 g

Serves: 4
Active prep time: 10 minutes
Cook time: 7 minutes

1 pound ground beef (80% lean)
3 tablespoons crushed pork rinds
1 large egg
½ teaspoon chipotle powder
¼ teaspoon garlic powder
¼ teaspoon onion powder
⅛ teaspoon ground cumin
1 (8 ounce) can tomato sauce
2 teaspoons taco seasoning
¼ teaspoon fine Himalayan pink salt
1 tablespoon avocado oil
1 head butter lettuce, separated into leaves
Toppings, such as sour cream, shredded cheese, diced avocado, fresh cilantro

For the Quick Pickled Onions:
⅓ cup thinly sliced red onions
2 tablespoons rice vinegar
Squeeze of fresh lime juice
Pinch of fine Himalayan pink salt

Double Mustard–Dill Pickle Pot Roast

If you like Mississippi pot roast, you will love this equally briny and flavorful dish. Using both fresh and dried dill as well as dill pickles ensures you get that essential dill flavor in every bite, and a good shot of pickle juice helps to tenderize the meat. Serve this savory roast with a side of creamy mashed cauliflower made with butter and heavy cream, or Creamed Brussels Sprouts with Bacon (page 69). Yum!

Serves: 4
Active prep time: 10 minutes
Cook time: 60 minutes

2 teaspoons yellow mustard seeds
1 teaspoon dried dill
1 teaspoon fine Himalayan pink salt
½ teaspoon black pepper
2½- to 3-pound beef chuck roast
2 tablespoons olive oil
1 stalk celery, chopped
1 small onion, chopped
2 cloves garlic, chopped
½ cup sliced kosher dill pickles
½ cup kosher dill pickle juice
1 tablespoon Dijon mustard
1 tablespoon chopped fresh dill

1. In a small bowl, combine the mustard seeds, dried dill, pink salt, and pepper. Press the mixture evenly onto the roast.

2. Select **SAUTÉ** on the Instant Pot. When the pot is hot, add the olive oil. Add the roast to the hot oil and cook until browned, about 10 minutes, turning as needed to brown on all sides. (The seeds will pop!) Remove the roast from the pot. Add the celery, onion, and garlic. Cook and stir for 2 minutes. Return the roast to the pot. Add the pickles and pickle juice. Select **CANCEL**.

3. Secure the lid on the pot and close the pressure-release valve. Set the pot to **HIGH** pressure for 60 minutes. At the end of the cooking time, use a natural release to depressurize. Transfer the roast from the pot to a serving dish.

4. Whisk the Dijon mustard into the cooking liquid in the pot. Select **SAUTÉ** and simmer until the gravy is slightly thickened, 5 to 10 minutes. Select **CANCEL**. Stir in the fresh dill.

5. Serve the roast on a platter with the gravy.

Per serving: Calories: 701 • Total Fat: 50 g • Protein: 56 g • Total Carbs: 4 g • Fiber: 1 g • Erythritol: 0 g • Net Carbs: 3 g

Short Rib Ragu

Rich and indulgent, short ribs are definitely a go-to comfort food for me, and they happen to be one of my favorite cuts of beef. Short ribs take time to prepare properly—you want them to be fall-off-the-bone tender—but the Instant Pot speeds things up considerably. Instead of taking all day to slow-roast in the oven, these short ribs can be on your dinner table in a little over an hour.

1. In a small bowl, combine the garlic powder, pink salt, and pepper. Sprinkle the mixture over all sides of the short ribs.

2. Select **SAUTÉ** on the Instant Pot. When the pot is hot, add the olive oil. Add the short ribs to the hot oil, taking care not to over-crowd the pot. If necessary, cook in two batches. Brown on all sides, rendering the fat as well, 6 to 8 minutes. Select **CANCEL**. Transfer the ribs to a platter and cover with foil.

3. Pour off all but about 2 tablespoons oil from the pot. Select **SAUTÉ**. When the pot is hot, add the mushrooms and onion. Cook for 3 minutes or until the vegetables have softened. Select **CANCEL**. Stir in the tomatoes, bay leaf, rosemary, and oregano. Return the short ribs to the pot.

4. Secure the lid on the pot and close the pressure-release valve. Set the pot to **HIGH** pressure for 45 minutes. At the end of the cooking time, use a natural release to depressurize for 10 minutes, then quick-release the remaining pressure.

5. Transfer the ribs to a serving dish. Remove the bay leaf and discard. If desired, thicken the cooking juices into a gravy by stirring the coconut flour into the liquid left in the pot.

Serves: 4
Active prep time: 10 minutes
Cook time: 45 minutes

1 teaspoon garlic powder
1 teaspoon fine Himalayan pink salt
1 teaspoon black pepper
4 beef short ribs (about 2 pounds total)
1 tablespoon olive oil
2 cups quartered mushrooms
½ cup diced red onion
1 (15-ounce) can crushed tomatoes
1 bay leaf
1 teaspoon dried rosemary
½ teaspoon dried oregano
1 tablespoon coconut flour (optional)

Per serving: Calories: 380 • Total Fat: 22 g • Protein: 35 g • Total Carbs: 11 g • Fiber: 3 g • Erythritol: 0 g • Net Carbs: 8 g

Steak Roll-Ups with Shiitake Mushroom Sauce

This is a beautiful dish that looks impressive on the plate and pairs a classic duo—steak and asparagus—with an Asian-inspired mushroom sauce made with fresh ginger, garlic, sesame oil, and tamari. These steak roll-ups are super high in protein and low in carbs, making them a great option no matter where you are on your keto journey. For a complete meal, serve them with my Cauliflower Fried Rice (page 66).

Serves: 2
Active prep time: 20 minutes
Cook time: 7 minutes

1 pound round steak
½ teaspoon fine Himalayan pink salt, divided
½ teaspoon black pepper
8 thin asparagus spears, trimmed and halved crosswise
4 thick green onions, roots and top 2 inches of the green trimmed; they should be equal in length to your asparagus spears
3 tablespoons avocado oil, divided
2 tablespoons minced shallot
1 tablespoon minced fresh ginger
1 clove garlic, minced
1 cup sliced shiitake mushroom caps
1 cup beef broth
2 tablespoons coconut aminos, tamari, or soy sauce
Toasted sesame seeds
Toasted sesame oil, for drizzling (optional)

1. Place the round steak in the freezer for 30 minutes (to make slicing easier). Cut the steak against the grain into 8 pieces. Gently pound each piece to a ¼ inch thickness. Use ¼ teaspoon each of the pink salt and pepper to season one side of all the pieces. Place 2 asparagus spears and 1 green onion on the beef and roll up to enclose. Secure with a toothpick. Sprinkle all the rolls with the remaining ¼ teaspoon each salt and black pepper.

2. Select **SAUTÉ** on the Instant Pot. When the pot is hot, add 1 tablespoon of the avocado oil. Add four of the rolls to the hot oil and cook until browned, about 2 minutes. Turn and cook an additional 2 minutes to brown on the second side. Transfer the rolls to a plate. Repeat with the remaining rolls and 1 tablespoon oil.

3. Add the remaining 1 tablespoon oil to the pot. Add the shallot, ginger, and garlic and cook for 1 minute, then add the mushrooms. Cook, stirring frequently, until the mushrooms are browned, about 3 minutes. Add the broth and coconut aminos and scrape the bottom of the pot to loosen any browned bits. Select **CANCEL**. Return the rolls to the pot.

4. Secure the lid on the pot and close the pressure-release valve. Set the pot to **HIGH** pressure for 7 minutes. At the end of the cooking time, quick-release the pressure.

5. Remove the rolls from the pot and cover to keep warm. Select **SAUTÉ** and bring the cooking liquid to a boil. Simmer for 5 minutes to reduce slightly. Select **CANCEL**.

6. Ladle the mushroom sauce over the rolls. Sprinkle with sesame seeds and, if desired, drizzle with sesame oil.

Per serving: Calories: 518 • Total Fat: 27 g • Protein: 60 g • Total Carbs: 12 g • Fiber: 4 g • Erythritol: 0 g • Net Carbs: 8 g

Enchilada Meatballs

Think enchilada sauce is just for tortillas? Think again! In this dish, a rich, smoky sauce made with chipotle peppers creates a pool of flavor for tender beef meatballs. I like to serve these meatballs with a Mexican-inspired salad made with romaine, cucumbers, radish, toasted pumpkin seeds, and a sprinkle of queso fresco.

10 INGREDIENTS OR LESS

Serves: 4
Active prep time: 10 minutes
Cook time: 5 minutes

1 pound ground beef (80–85% lean)
½ cup crumbled queso fresco, feta cheese, or shredded Mexican blend cheese, divided
⅓ cup almond flour
¼ cup chopped green onion
1 large egg, lightly beaten
1 to 2 teaspoons chile-lime seasoning (such as Tajín), to taste
2 tablespoons butter or ghee, divided
1 (19-ounce) can red enchilada sauce
1 chipotle pepper in adobo sauce, chopped, plus 1 tablespoon adobo sauce
1 tablespoon chopped fresh cilantro

1. In a medium bowl, combine the beef, ¼ cup of the cheese, the almond flour, green onion, egg, and chili-lime seasoning. Mix until thoroughly combined. Roll the meat mixture into 12 meatballs.

2. Select SAUTÉ on the Instant Pot. When the pot is hot, add 1 tablespoon of the butter. Add half of the meatballs to the hot butter and cook until browned (the meatballs will not be cooked through), 3 to 4 minutes. Transfer the meatballs to a bowl. Repeat with the remaining meatballs and 1 tablespoon butter. Select CANCEL. Return all the meatballs to the pot. Add the enchilada sauce, chipotle pepper, and adobo sauce.

3. Secure the lid on the pot and close the pressure-release valve. Set the pot to HIGH pressure for 5 minutes. At the end of the cooking time, quick-release the pressure.

4. Sprinkle with the remaining ¼ cup cheese and the cilantro, and serve.

Per serving: Calories: 453 • Total Fat: 34 g • Protein: 28 g • Total Carbs: 9 g • Fiber: 2 g • Erythritol: 0 g • Net Carbs: 7 g

Gyro Tzatziki Bowl

Tzatziki is a cool, creamy Greek yogurt sauce made with cucumbers, dill, and fresh garlic. I could eat it on just about anything. It's the perfect accompaniment to many Mediterranean dishes, including this keto-friendly "gyro" bowl. I like to top my bowl with black olives, feta, onion, and sliced pepperoncini for that true "gyro" experience, but feel free to get creative with your own favorite toppings. My Quick Pickled Onions (page 167) would also be delicious here!

1. Pour 1 cup water into the Instant Pot. Place 2 layers of foil on a trivet with handles, leaving enough space around the edges for steam to circulate. Brush the foil lightly with olive oil.

2. In a food processor, combine the ground meat, onion, garlic, fresh oregano, dried oregano, 1 teaspoon pink salt, and 1 teaspoon pepper. Pulse several times, then puree until smooth. Form into an oval loaf and place on the foil-lined trivet. Place the trivet in the pot.

3. Secure the lid on the pot and close the pressure-release valve. Set the pot to **HIGH** pressure for 15 minutes. At the end of the cooking time, use a natural release to depressurize.

4. Carefully remove the loaf from the pot. Let cool for at least 15 minutes. Cut the loaf into ¼-inch-thick slices.

5. Adjust an oven rack to 6 inches below the heat source. Preheat the broiler. Line a large baking sheet with foil. Brush the foil with olive oil. Transfer the meat slices to the prepared sheet and broil until browned, 2 to 3 minutes. Flip the slices and broil until browned, 2 to 3 minutes more.

6. Meanwhile, make the tzatziki: In a small bowl, combine the yogurt, cucumber, dill, and garlic. Season the tzatziki to taste with pink salt and pepper.

7. Place the lettuce in serving bowls. Top with the meat, tzatziki, sliced red onion, feta, and pepperoncini.

Per serving: Calories: 511 • Total Fat: 32 g • Protein: 42 g • Total Carbs: 13 g • Fiber: 3 g • Erythritol: 0 g • Net Carbs: 10 g

Serves: 4
Active prep time: 20 minutes
Cook time: 15 minutes

Olive oil, for brushing
1½ pounds ground beef or lamb
¼ cup chopped onion
2 cloves garlic, chopped
1 tablespoon chopped fresh oregano
1 teaspoon dried oregano
Fine Himalayan pink salt
Black pepper

For the tzatziki:
¾ cup plain Greek yogurt (you could also use sour cream if desired)
½ cup shredded cucumber
1½ teaspoons chopped fresh dill
1 clove garlic, minced

2 romaine hearts, chopped
1 small red onion, thinly sliced, for serving
1 cup crumbled feta cheese, for serving
Sliced pepperoncini peppers, for serving (optional)

Spinach and Mozzarella-Stuffed Meatballs

These cheese-filled meatballs are a hit with kids and adults alike—and the best part is, they come together in minutes, using ingredients you probably already have in your fridge. I use frozen spinach for these meatballs, but if you have fresh on hand, you could quickly wilt it on the stovetop or in the microwave. For a spicier meatball, replace half the ground beef with hot Italian sausage.

Serves: 4

Active prep time: 15 minutes

Cook time: 7 minutes

½ cup frozen chopped spinach, thawed

1 pound ground beef (80% lean)

⅓ cup almond flour

1 large egg, lightly beaten

¼ cup finely chopped onion

¼ cup grated Parmesan cheese (1 ounce)

4 teaspoons Italian seasoning, divided

2 mozzarella cheese sticks, each cut into 4 pieces

1 (24-ounce) jar no-sugar-added marinara sauce (like Rao's)

⅓ cup sliced Kalamata or black olives

¼ cup chopped fresh Italian parsley or basil

1. Place the spinach in a fine-mesh sieve set over a bowl. Press with a large spoon to remove the liquid (discard the liquid).

2. In a large bowl, combine the spinach, beef, almond flour, egg, onion, Parmesan, and 2 teaspoons of the Italian seasoning. Gently mix the meat mixture until well combined. Shape into 8 meatballs. With your thumb, push a piece of cheese stick into the center of each meatball and reshape the meatball.

3. Pour half of the marinara sauce into the Instant Pot. Top with the meatballs, olives, and remaining 2 teaspoons Italian seasoning. Cover with the remaining marinara sauce.

4. Secure the lid on the pot and close the pressure-release valve. Set the pot to **HIGH** pressure for 7 minutes. At the end of the cooking time, quick-release the pressure.

5. Serve the meatballs topped with sauce and a sprinkle of parsley or basil.

Per serving: Calories: 480 • Total Fat: 34 g • Protein: 33 g • Total Carbs: 11 g • Fiber: 2 g • Erythritol: 0 g • Net Carbs: 9 g

Three-Cheese Philly Cheesesteak Casserole

To be 100 percent honest with you, I've never had an actual Philly cheesesteak sandwich, so loyalists, be warned: This is my keto-friendly *imagining* of the cult classic. That said, in terms of capturing the flavors of the beloved sandwich (minus the bread), I hope I nailed it. I like to top mine with thinly sliced banana peppers, hot sauce, and sliced olives.

1. Grease a 7-inch round baking dish with 1 tablespoon of the butter.

2. Season the meat with ½ teaspoon each of the pink salt and pepper. Select **SAUTÉ** on the Instant Pot. Add 1 tablespoon of the butter. Add half of the steak to the hot butter and cook, stirring occasionally, until the meat is browned, about 10 minutes. Use a slotted spoon to transfer the meat to a bowl. Repeat with the remaining meat and 1 tablespoon butter.

3. Add the mushrooms, bell pepper, onion, and oregano to the pot. Cook, stirring occasionally, until softened and the liquid has evaporated, about 10 minutes. Stir in the meat and cook 2 minutes more. Select **CANCEL**. Stir in the Parmesan. Add the provolone and American cheeses and stir to combine. Transfer the mixture to the greased baking dish.

4. In a medium bowl, whisk together the cream and eggs. Whisk in the remaining ½ teaspoon each salt and pepper. Pour the eggs over the mixture in the baking dish. Cover the dish tightly with foil.

5. Clean the pot if you wish. Pour 1 cup water into the pot. Place a trivet with handles in the pot and place the baking dish on the trivet.

6. Secure the lid on the pot and close the pressure-release valve. Set the pot to **HIGH** pressure for 20 minutes. At the end of the cooking time, use a natural release to depressurize. Let stand 10 minutes before serving.

Per serving: Calories: 915 • Total Fat: 75 g • Protein: 52 g • Total Carbs: 10 g • Fiber: 2 g • Erythritol: 0 g • Net Carbs: 8 g

Serves: 4
Active prep time: 15 minutes
Cook time: 20 minutes

3 tablespoons butter or ghee, divided

1½ pounds rib eye or sirloin steak, thinly sliced, cut into bite-size pieces

1 teaspoon fine Himalayan pink salt, divided

1 teaspoon black pepper, divided

8 ounces sliced button mushrooms

1 green bell pepper, sliced

1 medium yellow onion, sliced

1 teaspoon dried oregano, crushed

½ cup grated Parmesan cheese (2 ounces), plus more for garnish

1 cup shredded provolone cheese (4 ounces)

4 slices American cheese, chopped

½ cup heavy cream

2 large eggs

Italian Shredded Beef

On a cold winter day, there's nothing like a hearty bowl of this Italian shredded beef to warm you up. This rich, savory dish absolutely melts in your mouth and tastes like it's been cooked for hours. For a complete meal, I like to serve this beef with a side of my Spicy Bacon Green Bean Toss (page 74), though you could also serve it over cauliflower rice or with a simple green salad.

Serves: 4

Active prep time: 20 minutes

Cook time: 50 minutes

2 pounds boneless beef chuck roast, trimmed, cut into 2-inch chunks

1 teaspoon fine Himalayan pink salt

1 teaspoon black pepper

2 tablespoons olive oil

1 cup sliced yellow onion

1 tablespoon minced garlic

2 tablespoons tomato paste

1 tablespoon Italian seasoning

1 cup beef broth

2 bay leaves

1 tablespoon balsamic vinegar

1½ cups shredded provolone or mozzarella cheese (6 ounces)

¼ cup sliced pepperoncini peppers

1. Season the beef chunks on all sides with the pink salt and black pepper. Select SAUTÉ on the Instant Pot. When the pot is hot, add the olive oil. Add the beef in a single layer to the hot oil and sear, turning, until browned all over, about 6 to 8 minutes. Remove the beef and set aside.

2. Add the onion and garlic to the pot and cook, stirring often, until the onion begins to soften and brown, about 3 minutes. Stir in the tomato paste and Italian seasoning and cook until the paste darkens slightly, about 2 minutes. Add the beef broth and scrape the bottom of the pot to loosen any browned bits. Add the bay leaves to the pot and return the beef to the pot. Select CANCEL.

3. Secure the lid on the pot and close the pressure-release valve. Set the pot to HIGH pressure for 50 minutes. At the end of the cooking time, quick-release the pressure.

4. Transfer the meat to a cutting board. Discard the bay leaves. Use two forks to shred the beef, then return the meat to the pot. Stir in the balsamic vinegar. Sprinkle the cheese on the beef and cover the pot with the lid. Let stand, covered, until the cheese melts.

5. Spoon into bowls and top each serving with some of the pepperoncini.

Per serving: Calories: 729 • Total Fat: 51 g • Protein: 56 g • Total Carbs: 9 g • Fiber: 2 g • Erythritol: 0 g • Net Carbs: 7 g

Ginger and Five-Spice Brisket Bowls

Made from cinnamon, cloves, fennel, star anise, and Sichuan peppercorns, five-spice powder is a Chinese seasoning blend that includes sweet, sour, bitter, salty, and umami notes. It adds a lot of flavor and a little heat to any dish. Here I've paired it with fresh ginger to create a brisket seasoning unlike anything you've ever tasted—and the whole meal has only 8 grams of net carbs. As with all of my bowls, I'm crazy about the toppings—for this one, I like to add sliced radishes, fresh basil, and thinly sliced avocado.

1. Sprinkle the beef on all sides with the garlic salt and black pepper to taste. Select **SAUTÉ** on the Instant Pot. When the pot is hot, add the avocado oil. Add the beef to the hot oil and cook until browned, about 6 minutes. Add the broth, ginger, coconut aminos, and five-spice powder to the pot. Select **CANCEL**.

2. Secure the lid on the pot and close the pressure-release valve. Set the pot to **HIGH** pressure for 20 minutes. At the end of the cooking time, quick-release the pressure.

3. In a large bowl, toss the fennel with the vinegar and sesame oil. Divide among four serving bowls. Use a slotted spoon to add the beef to the bowls. Drizzle with some of the cooking juices, and serve, with toppings if desired.

Per serving: Calories: 677 • Total Fat: 50 g • Protein: 44 g • Total Carbs: 12 g • Fiber: 4 g • Erythritol: 0 g • Net Carbs: 8 g

Serves: 2
Active prep time: 15 minutes
Cook time: 20 minutes

1 to 1½ pounds beef brisket, trimmed and cut into bite-size pieces, or beef stew meat
1 teaspoon garlic salt
Black pepper
1 tablespoon avocado oil
1 cup beef broth
1 tablespoon grated fresh ginger
2 tablespoons coconut aminos, tamari, or soy sauce
1 teaspoon five-spice powder
1 large fennel bulb, thinly sliced, or 4 cups thinly sliced napa cabbage
2 tablespoons rice vinegar
1 teaspoon toasted sesame oil
Sliced radish (optional)
Sliced avocado (optional)

Sweets

Cinnamon-Pecan Coffee Cake

Growing up, my favorite breakfast was a boxed coffee cake that my mom would make. We would add chopped pecans to the top and slather it in butter—it was just incredible. This keto-friendly version of one of my favorite childhood treats is just as delicious as I remember. In the fall I sometimes like to change up the flavor by swapping pumpkin pie spice for the cinnamon, and walnuts or almonds for the pecans—either way, you won't be able to eat just one slice!

1. Coat a 7-inch round baking dish with the 1 tablespoon softened butter. In a small bowl, stir together ½ cup of the erythritol brown sugar, ¼ cup of the heavy cream, and the pecans. Spoon into the prepared dish to cover the bottom. Set aside.

2. In a small bowl, stir together the remaining ¼ cup erythritol brown sugar, ¼ cup of the coconut flour, 2 tablespoons of the melted butter, the cinnamon, and ⅛ teaspoon of the pink salt. Set the cinnamon mixture aside.

3. In a medium bowl, combine the almond flour, remaining ½ cup coconut flour, the granular erythritol, baking powder, and remaining ⅛ teaspoon pink salt. Create a well in the center of the dry ingredients. Add the eggs, sour cream, vanilla, and the remaining 3 tablespoons melted butter and ¼ cup heavy cream. Stir the batter until smooth.

4. Drop half of the batter in small mounds on the pecan mixture in the baking dish. Sprinkle the cinnamon mixture over the batter. Drop the remaining batter in small mounds on the cinnamon mixture. Cover the dish tightly with foil.

5. Pour 2 cups water into the Instant Pot. Place a trivet with handles in the pot and place the dish on the trivet. Secure the lid on the pot and close the pressure-release valve. Set the pot to **HIGH** pressure for 30 minutes. At the end of the cooking time, use a natural release to depressurize.

6. Transfer the dish to a wire rack and let stand for 5 minutes. Remove the foil and invert the cake onto a serving plate. Cut into slices and serve.

Serves: 6
Active prep time: 20 minutes
Cook time: 30 minutes

5 tablespoons butter or ghee, melted, plus 1 tablespoon softened butter, divided
¾ cup erythritol brown sugar replacement, divided
½ cup heavy cream, divided
½ cup chopped toasted pecans
¾ cup coconut flour, divided
2 teaspoons ground cinnamon
¼ teaspoon fine Himalayan pink salt, divided
1 cup almond flour
¼ cup granular erythritol
1 teaspoon baking powder
2 large eggs
¼ cup sour cream
1 teaspoon vanilla extract

Per serving: Calories: 446 • Total Fat: 40 g • Protein: 10 g • Total Carbs: 47 g • Fiber: 8 g • Erythritol: 32 g • Net Carbs: 7 g

Mini Pudding Cakes with Blackberry Puree

Ramekin cakes are one of my go-to treats when I'm craving something sweet—they're the perfect portion and cook so easily in a pressure cooker. The steamed, moist texture of this vanilla cake is lovely and pairs well with all kinds of berries—strawberries, blueberries, or raspberries.

10 INGREDIENTS OR LESS

Serves: 4
Active prep time: 15 minutes
Cook time: 10 minutes

1 tablespoon butter or ghee, at room temperature
²⁄₃ cup plus 2 teaspoons granular erythritol, divided
¹⁄₃ cup almond flour
½ teaspoon grated nutmeg
Pinch of fine Himalayan pink salt
½ cup canned coconut milk
2 large eggs, separated
Grated zest and juice of 1 lime
½ teaspoon vanilla extract
1 cup blackberries

1. Lightly grease four 5- to 6-ounce ramekins with the butter. Sprinkle each ramekin with ¼ teaspoon erythritol to lightly coat. Set aside.

2. In a medium bowl, stir together the ²⁄₃ cup erythritol, almond flour, nutmeg, and pink salt. In a small bowl, stir together the coconut milk, egg yolks, 1 tablespoon of the lime juice, and the vanilla. Stir the egg yolk mixture into the almond flour mixture just until combined.

3. In a small bowl, with an electric mixer, beat the egg whites until stiff peaks form (tips stand straight). Gently fold the egg whites into the batter. Spoon the batter into the ramekins. Cover each ramekin with a piece of foil lightly coated with cooking spray.

4. Pour 1 cup hot water into the Instant Pot. Place a trivet with handles in the pot and arrange three ramekins on the trivet. Stagger the remaining ramekin on top of the others.

5. Secure the lid on the pot and close the pressure-release valve. Set the pot to **HIGH** pressure for 10 minutes. At the end of the cooking time, quick-release the pressure. Let the ramekins stand in the pot with the lid on for 10 minutes. Carefully transfer the ramekins to a wire rack, remove the foil, and let cool for 15 minutes.

6. Meanwhile, make the blackberry puree: In a blender or food processor, combine the blackberries and the remaining erythritol. Process until smooth. Strain the puree through a fine-mesh strainer set over a bowl, using the back of a spoon to press the puree and remove the seeds.

7. Invert the ramekins onto serving dishes. Sprinkle with lime zest and serve with the blackberry puree.

Per serving: Calories: 179 • Total Fat: 14 g • Protein: 6 g • Total Carbs: 41 g • Fiber: 3 g • Erythritol: 34 g • Net Carbs: 4 g

Mini Chocolate-Espresso Lava Cakes with Sea Salt

This dessert is a chocolate lover's dream, especially if (like me) you're someone who enjoys the combination of salty and sweet. Just a small sprinkle of a flaky sea salt on top of this cake is all you need to get that perfect bite. Add a few fresh raspberries or strawberries and a dollop of slightly sweetened whipped cream or coconut cream for true indulgence with only 4 grams of net carbs!

1. Brush two 5- to 6-ounce ramekins with the softened butter.

2. In a medium bowl, combine the melted butter and the cocoa powder. Stir in the erythritol, espresso powder, baking powder, and salt. Whisk in the egg and vanilla. Spoon the batter into the prepared ramekins. Cover the ramekins tightly with foil that has been coated with cooking spray.

3. Pour 1 cup water into the Instant Pot. Place a trivet with handles in the pot and place the filled ramekins on the trivet. Secure the lid on the pot and close the pressure-release valve. Set the pot to **HIGH** pressure for 9 minutes. At the end of the cooking time, quick-release the pressure.

4. Uncover the pot and let the cakes cool in the pot for 10 minutes. Carefully remove the ramekins from the pot, remove the foil, and let sit for 5 minutes. Serve warm, sprinkled with flaky sea salt.

Pressure Cooker Tip: Simple and inexpensive, a canning jar lifter makes it safe and easy to remove ramekins from the pot.

Per serving: Calories: 332 • Total Fat: 34 g • Protein: 5 g • Total Carbs: 26 g • Fiber: 4 g • Erythritol: 18 g • Net Carbs: 4 g

10 INGREDIENTS OR LESS

Serves: 2
Active prep time: 10 minutes
Cook time: 9 minutes

1 to 2 tablespoons butter or ghee, softened, plus 4 tablespoons, melted
¼ cup unsweetened cocoa powder
3 tablespoons granular erythritol
2 teaspoons instant espresso powder (or dark roast instant coffee)
½ teaspoon baking powder
Pinch of fine Himalayan pink salt
1 large egg
½ teaspoon vanilla extract
½ to 1 teaspoon flaky sea salt, to taste

Spice Cake with Lemon Drizzle

Bundt cakes are some of my favorite desserts to make—I love how pretty they look on a table. This incredible-smelling cake made with pumpkin pie spice is brightened up by a fresh lemon icing that really brings the whole thing together. Try topping the cake with a handful of toasted chopped pecans to add crunch and nutty flavor.

Serves: 6
Active prep time: 15 minutes
Cook time: 25 minutes

Butter or ghee, for the baking dish
1½ cups almond flour
⅓ cup granular erythritol
1½ teaspoons baking powder
1½ teaspoons pumpkin pie spice
⅛ teaspoon fine Himalayan pink salt
2 large eggs, lightly beaten
4 tablespoons butter or ghee, melted
3 tablespoons heavy cream
¾ teaspoon vanilla extract

For the lemon drizzle:

2 tablespoons powdered erythritol
1 teaspoon grated lemon zest
¼ teaspoon fresh lemon juice
¼ teaspoon vanilla extract

1. Generously grease a 3-cup tube pan with butter. In a medium bowl, stir together the almond flour, erythritol, baking powder, pumpkin pie spice, and pink salt. Create a well in the center of the dry ingredients and add the eggs, melted butter, cream, and vanilla. Stir the dry and wet ingredients together until smooth. Pour the batter into the prepared pan.

2. Pour 1 cup water into the Instant Pot. Place a trivet with handles in the pot and place the tube pan on the trivet. Secure the lid on the pot and close the pressure-release valve. Set the pot to **HIGH** pressure for 25 minutes. At the end of the cooking time, quick-release the pressure. Transfer the cake to a wire rack to cool for 10 minutes. Invert the cake onto the wire rack and let cool completely.

3. Meanwhile, make the lemon drizzle: In a small bowl, combine the powdered erythritol, lemon zest, lemon juice, vanilla, and ¼ teaspoon water. Stir until drizzling consistency. Drizzle over the cooled cake.

Per serving: Calories: 335 • Total Fat: 32 g • Protein: 8 g • Total Carbs: 21 g • Fiber: 3 g • Erythritol: 15 • Net Carbs: 3 g

Vanilla Bean Cheesecake

A ten-ingredient cheesecake with only 5 grams of net carbs? No, you're not dreaming! While this cheesecake may seem too good to be true, it's a breeze to make in the pressure cooker—and the texture is smooth as silk. If you can't find a fresh vanilla bean, you can add a little extra vanilla extract—but the fresh vanilla imparts a flavor that makes this cake truly special. The hardest part is waiting for it to chill, but your patience will be rewarded!

1. To prevent the crust from getting soggy, cut a piece of foil the same size as a piece of paper towel. Cover the foil with the paper towel and set a 6-inch springform pan on the paper towel. Bring up the edges of the foil. Make sure you don't skip this step because no one likes a soggy crust on their cheesecake!

2. In small bowl, combine the almond flour and 1 tablespoon erythritol. Add the melted butter and stir until combined. Press the mixture into the bottom of the pan.

3. In a large bowl, with an electric mixer, beat the cream cheese for 30 seconds. Scrape the seeds from the vanilla bean into the bowl. Add the ⅔ cup erythritol and beat at medium speed until combined. Beat in the eggs and cream. Beat in the lemon zest, lemon juice, and vanilla. Pour the batter over the crust.

4. Pour 1 cup water into the Instant Pot. Place a trivet with handles in the pot and place the cheesecake on the trivet. Cover the cheesecake with a piece of foil. Secure the lid on the pot and close the pressure-release valve. Set the pot to **HIGH** pressure for 45 minutes. At the end of the cooking time, use a natural release to depressurize for 15 minutes, then quick-release the remaining pressure.

5. Carefully remove the pan and trivet. Remove the foil/paper towel from the outside of the pan. Let the cheesecake cool on a wire rack for 1 hour. Cover and refrigerate for at least 4 and up to 24 hours. Run a knife around the cheesecake, then loosen and remove the sides.

10 INGREDIENTS OR LESS

Serves: 6
Active prep time: 15 minutes
Cook time: 45 minutes

¾ cup almond flour
⅔ cup plus 1 tablespoon granular erythritol, divided
2 tablespoons butter or ghee, melted
12 ounces cream cheese, at room temperature
1 vanilla bean, split lengthwise
3 large eggs
¼ cup heavy cream
1 teaspoon grated lemon zest
2 teaspoons fresh lemon juice
1 teaspoon vanilla extract

Per serving: Calories: 386 • Total Fat: 37 g • Protein: 10 g • Total Carbs: 30 g • Fiber: 2 g • Erythritol: 23 g • Net Carbs: 5 g

Matcha-Coconut Custard

Matcha is a fine powder made from ground green tea leaves. It's become incredibly popular lately, both in cafe-style drinks (like lattes) and baked goods. Personally, I love all things matcha—it has such a complex, slightly nutty flavor with a hint of sweetness, plus it's full of antioxidants and incredibly good for you. Serve these pretty green custards with a little whipped cream or coconut cream, fresh blackberries, and a sprinkle of toasted pistachio nuts for a stunning presentation.

10 INGREDIENTS OR LESS

Serves: 4
Active prep time: 15 minutes
Cook time: 15 minutes

1 (13.5- to 15-ounce) can coconut milk, depending on brand
2 teaspoons matcha powder or 3 green tea bags
¾ cup granular erythritol
3 large eggs, lightly beaten
1 teaspoon vanilla extract
Grated nutmeg, for serving
Toasted pistachios, for serving

1. Select **SAUTÉ** on the Instant Pot. Add the coconut milk and heat just until hot but not boiling, 2 to 3 minutes. Select **CANCEL**. If using matcha, whisk into the coconut milk until well combined. If using tea bags, add them to the hot coconut milk and let stand 5 minutes. Gently press the bags with the back of a spoon to release more tea, then discard the tea bags. Pour the tea-infused milk into a medium bowl and let cool for 5 minutes. Wash the pot.

2. Add the erythritol, eggs, and vanilla to the tea/milk mixture and whisk until well combined but not foamy. Ladle the egg mixture into four ungreased 6-ounce ramekins. Cover each ramekin tightly with foil.

3. Pour 1 cup hot water into the Instant Pot. Place a trivet with handles in the pot. Place three ramekins on the trivet, then stagger the remaining ramekin on top.

4. Secure the lid on the pot and close the pressure-release valve. Set the pot to **HIGH** pressure for 12 minutes. At the end of the cooking time, use a natural release to depressurize for 6 minutes, then quick-release any remaining pressure. The custards are done if a knife inserted near the center comes out clean.

5. Carefully remove the ramekins from the pot. Cool for 30 minutes on a wire rack. Refrigerate until chilled, at least 2 hours or up to 2 days. Just before serving, sprinkle with nutmeg or toasted pistachios.

Per serving: Calories: 218 • Total Fat: 18 g • Protein: 6 g •
Total Carbs: 15 g • Fiber: 0 g • Erythritol: 12 g • Net Carbs: 3 g

Fudgy Brownie Bites with Berries and Pecans

I like to use silicone egg bite molds to make these individual brownies, which are just the thing when you need something chocolatey, STAT. Once you get used to making the batter, these brownies can be customized in endless ways—one of my favorite variations is to add ¼ cup toasted unsweetened shredded coconut and ¼ cup canned coconut milk to the batter in place of the berries and nuts. I recommend doubling the recipe and stashing half a dozen of these bites in the freezer for emergency chocolate cravings!

Serves: 6
Active prep time: 10 minutes
Cook time: 7 minutes

¾ cup sliced strawberries, divided
¾ cup sliced blackberries, divided
4 tablespoons butter or ghee, at room temperature
2 ounces cream cheese, at room temperature
⅔ cup almond flour
½ cup unsweetened cocoa powder
½ teaspoon baking powder
¼ teaspoon fine Himalayan pink salt
1 large egg, lightly beaten
1 teaspoon vanilla extract
2 tablespoons finely chopped pecans
1 teaspoon grated orange zest

1. In a small bowl, combine ¼ cup each of the strawberries and blackberries and mash with a fork. Set aside.

2. In a medium bowl, with an electric mixer, combine the butter, cream cheese, almond flour, cocoa powder, baking powder, pink salt, egg, and vanilla. Add the mashed berries and their juice. Mix on medium speed until well combined. Stir in the pecans.

3. Pour 1 cup water into the Instant Pot. Place a trivet with handles in the pot. Press the brownie batter into 6 cups of a silicone egg bite mold and place the mold on the trivet. Cover the mold with a paper towel and then foil.

4. Secure the lid on the pot and close the pressure-release valve. Set the pot to HIGH pressure for 7 minutes. At the end of the cooking time, quick-release the pressure. Carefully remove the trivet and egg mold from the pot. Uncover and invert the mold onto a wire rack.

5. While the brownies are cooling, in a small bowl, combine the remaining ½ cup each strawberries and blackberries. Serve the fruit with the brownie bites, sprinkled with the orange zest.

Per serving: Calories: 234 · Total Fat: 21 g · Protein: 6 g · Total Carbs: 11 g · Fiber: 5 g · Erythritol: 0 g · Net Carbs: 6 g

Lemon-Raspberry Cream Cheese Cake

This beautiful lemon-raspberry cream cheese cake is proof that you don't have to give up dessert when you go keto. Cream cheese combined with eggs and almond flour gives this cake a moist, dense texture that is luscious and even more satisfying than a traditional Bundt cake. You can ice it with the lemon cream cheese frosting for an impressive dessert, or simply slice and serve with a side of cream cheese for a special breakfast treat.

1. Generously coat a 3-cup Bundt pan with cooking spray.

2. In a medium bowl, with an electric mixer, beat the butter on medium speed for 30 seconds. Add the cream cheese and beat 1 minute more. Add the erythritol, baking powder, and pink salt. Beat 1 minute or until well combined. Add the eggs and beat well. Beat in the vanilla and lemon zest. Beat in the almond flour just until combined. Gently fold the raspberries into the batter. Spoon the batter into the pan.

3. Pour 1 cup water into the Instant Pot. Place a trivet with handles in the pot and place the pan on the trivet.

4. Secure the lid on the pot and close the pressure-release valve. Set the pot to HIGH pressure for 25 minutes. At the end of the cooking time, quick-release the pressure. Carefully remove the pan and trivet from the pot. Cool the cake in the pan on a wire rack for 10 minutes. Invert the cake onto the rack to cool completely.

5. Meanwhile, make the icing: In a small bowl, with an electric mixer, beat the cream cheese on medium speed for 30 seconds. Beat in the vanilla and lemon juice. Gradually beat in the powdered erythritol until smooth. Beat in water, 1 teaspoon at a time, until the icing is of drizzling consistency. Drizzle the cake with the icing. If desired, sprinkle with almonds.

Per serving: Calories: 451 · Total Fat: 44 g · Protein: 9 g · Total Carbs: 29 g · Fiber: 2 g · Erythritol: 21 g · Net Carbs: 6 g

Serves: 8
Active prep time: 15 minutes
Cook time: 25 minutes

¼ cup butter or ghee, at room temperature
7 tablespoons cream cheese, at room temperature
½ cup granular erythritol
½ teaspoon baking powder
¼ teaspoon fine Himalayan pink salt
2 large eggs, at room temperature, lightly beaten
1 teaspoon vanilla extract
1 teaspoon grated lemon zest
⅔ cup almond flour
½ cup raspberries

For the icing:
2 tablespoons cream cheese
1 teaspoon vanilla extract
1 teaspoon fresh lemon juice
¼ cup powdered erythritol

1 to 2 tablespoons sliced almonds toasted (optional)

Spiced Crème Brûlée

When I was a kid, my parents hosted holiday parties at our house, and the dessert spread always included mini crème brûlées. I absolutely loved them and it would not be an exaggeration to say that I probably ate a dozen in one night. When I changed my diet I was determined to find a way to make a keto-friendly version of this special treat. This spiced custard reminds me of the holidays, but if you prefer a classic crème brûlée, omit the cinnamon, nutmeg, and cloves and add one vanilla bean (split lengthwise) to the cream in step 1.

10 INGREDIENTS OR LESS

Serves: 4
Active prep time: 10 minutes
Cook time: 9 minutes

1½ cups heavy cream
¼ cup plus 4 teaspoons granular erythritol, divided
½ teaspoon ground cinnamon
¼ teaspoon grated nutmeg
⅛ teaspoon ground cloves
4 large egg yolks
1 teaspoon vanilla extract

1. In a small saucepan, heat the cream just until it starts to simmer. Remove from the heat and set aside to cool slightly.

2. Meanwhile, in a medium bowl, combine the ¼ cup erythritol, the cinnamon, nutmeg, and cloves. Whisk in the egg yolks and vanilla.

3. Slowly whisk the hot cream into the egg yolk mixture. Divide the custard mixture evenly among four 5- to 6-ounce ramekins or custard cups. Cover each dish tightly with foil.

4. Pour 1 cup water into the Instant Pot. Place a trivet with handles in the pot. Place three ramekins on the trivet, then stagger the remaining ramekin on top.

5. Secure the lid on the pot and close the pressure-release valve. Set the pot to HIGH pressure for 9 minutes. At the end of the cooking time, quick-release the pressure. Carefully remove the ramekins from the pot and let cool, covered, on a wire rack. Refrigerate for at least 2 hours or up to 8 hours.

6. Before serving, remove the foil from the ramekins and place them on a baking sheet. Adjust an oven rack so the tops of the ramekins are 4 inches from the heat source. Preheat the broiler. Sprinkle the top of each custard with 1 teaspoon erythritol. Broil until the tops are bubbling and lightly browned, 1 to 2 minutes (watch carefully to prevent burning). Remove from the oven and let sit until the topping hardens.

Per serving: Calories: 365 · Total Fat: 37 g · Protein: 5 g · Total Carbs: 20 g · Fiber: 0 g · Erythritol: 16 g · Net Carbs: 4 g

Dark Chocolate–Espresso Mousse with Mint Whipped Cream

Chocolate and coffee are two of my favorite things, so this rich mousse that incorporates both flavors ranks pretty high on my list of best things ever. The infusion of fresh mint paired with chocolate and coffee really takes things up a notch and makes this a guest-worthy dessert. If you don't have espresso powder on hand, you can use instant coffee (preferably dark roast) instead.

1. Grease the bottoms and sides of four 4-ounce ceramic ramekins with butter. Set aside.

2. In a medium bowl, whisk together the egg yolks and ¼ cup of the granular erythritol until thick and light yellow. Stir in 2 teaspoons of the vanilla.

3. In a microwave-safe bowl, stir together the chocolate, espresso powder, coconut milk, ¾ cup water, and remaining ¼ cup granular erythritol. Microwave for 1 minute at 50 percent power, then stir. Microwave at 50 percent power in 30-second increments, stirring after each, until the chocolate is melted.

4. Add a small amount of egg yolk mixture to the melted chocolate mixture and mix well. Then whisk the chocolate into the egg yolks. Pour into the prepared ramekins. Cover the ramekins with foil.

5. Pour 1 cup water into the Instant Pot. Place a trivet with handles in the pot. Place three ramekins on the trivet, then stagger the remaining ramekin on top. Secure the lid on the pot and close the pressure-release valve. Set the pot to **HIGH** pressure for 5 minutes. At the end of the cooking time, quick-release the pressure.

6. Carefully remove the ramekins. Let cool on a wire rack for 15 minutes, then refrigerate for at least 3 hours.

7. In a small saucepan, combine the mint leaves, ½ cup water, and the powdered erythritol. Bring to a boil over medium-high heat and let boil for 1 minute. Remove from the heat and let stand for 10 minutes. Strain out the leaves and let the syrup cool completely.

10 INGREDIENTS OR LESS

Serves: 4
Active prep time: 15 minutes
Cook time: 5 minutes

Butter or ghee, for the ramekins
4 large egg yolks
½ cup granular erythritol, divided
2¼ teaspoons vanilla extract, divided
2 ounces unsweetened chocolate, chopped
1 tablespoon espresso powder (or dark roast instant coffee)
¼ cup canned coconut milk
1 cup lightly packed fresh mint leaves, chopped, plus small leaves for garnish
2 tablespoons powdered erythritol
½ cup heavy cream

(continues)

8. In a bowl, with an electric mixer, beat the cream on high speed for 30 seconds. Slowly beat in 2 tablespoons of the minted syrup until stiff peaks form (tips stand straight). Fold in the remaining ¼ teaspoon vanilla.

9. Remove the foil from the ramekins. Top the mousse with whipped cream and additional fresh mint, if desired.

Per serving: Calories: 305 • Total Fat: 27 g • Protein: 6 g • Total Carbs: 37 g • Fiber: 2 g • Erythritol: 30 g • Net Carbs: 5 g

Acknowledgments

TO KAIA Having you as my daughter is my greatest joy. I love you to the moon and back, and I am beyond grateful to always have you by my side.

TO MY PARENTS I love you and thank you for allowing me to believe I could truly do anything if I worked hard enough.

TO MY FRIENDS AND FAMILY I am continuously inspired by my tribe, and I am very grateful to have such an amazing group of people around me. You are the people you surround yourself with, and I am lucky to be surrounded by greatness. To Julie and family, thank you for opening up your beautiful beachy dream home to me!

TO THE KETO COMMUNITY I am eternally grateful to have found the passionate and supportive keto community on Instagram and online. You are an incredible group of people, each fighting different challenges, but all trying to better yourselves. You all keep me accountable, and I hope I have been able to provide you with some delicious ways to live a ketogenic lifestyle.

TO MY KETO IN THE CITY FAMILY I started KITC alone with just me and an Instagram account, but over the last four years it has grown into much more with the help of some key people. Craig, thank you for your confidence in me and for helping me grow my passion for keto and food into so many wonderful opportunities. Chris and Carolyn, thank you for keeping me on track and for keeping ketointhecity.com thriving and growing.

TO MY BOOK FAMILY Andy Barzvi, you just never know who is going to reach out and change the course of your life. Thank you for believing in me and guiding me through this process. I am very thankful for your knowledge and expertise. To Julie Will and the whole HarperCollins team, it has been such a joy to be welcomed into your world. Thank you for your leadership and support bringing *Keto in an Instant* to life. Leslie Grow, Ashley Nevarez, and Kate Parisian, thank you for the gorgeous images and for bringing the food to a whole new level. Finally, to Ken, Lisa, and Tricia, thank you for testing, testing, and testing again, and making sure everything was just perfect!

Index

About the Author

JEN FISCH, creator of the blog *Keto in the City* and Instagram account @ketointhecity_, is passionate about offering simple solutions for following the ketogenic lifestyle. She is a single, working mother who has battled autoimmune disorders for twenty years and has turned to the kitchen to find simple, delicious ways to make the ketogenic diet work for her busy lifestyle.

Jen is not a nutritionist or trained chef, just a determined mom who searched high and low for a way of eating that would reduce the inflammation caused by her autoimmune disorders and allow her to feel like the very best version of herself.

Her first and second books, *The Easy 5-Ingredient Ketogenic Diet Cookbook* and *The Big Book of Ketogenic Diet Cooking*, are international best sellers. The recipes in both books were created to show people that keto can be delicious while also being very simple to make. Jen believes in using easy-to-find ingredients to make eating keto as attainable as possible.

She lives with her teenage daughter in Hermosa Beach, California.